The University Bible

Andrew Southwick

This first edition is published in 2013.

ALL RIGHTS RESERVED. This book contains material protected under International and Federal Copyright Laws and Treaties. Any unauthorized reprint or use of this material is prohibited. No part of this book may be reproduced or transmitted in any form or by any means, electronic or mechanical, including photocopying, recording, or by any information storage and retrieval system without express written permission from the author.

Copyright © Andrew Southwick 2013

ISBN-13: 978-1492185154

ISBN-10: 1492185159

Contents

About the author
Acknowledgements

Preface
Introduction

1. Choosing university
   Page 11

2. UCAS and Interviews
   Page 25

3. After the exam results
   Page 37

4. The first weekend
   Page 51

5. Induction week
   Page 77

6. Part-time jobs
   Page 85

7. Flatmates
   Page 97

8. Passing your course
   Page 113

9. Relationships
   Page 129

10. Mature Students
    Page 137

11. Through the good times and bad
    Page 141

About the author

Andrew Southwick graduated in 2011 from the University of the West of Scotland in BA Sports Journalism. He currently lives in Glasgow and works as a journalist for various broadcast and written media. In addition, he is also editor of his own website "The Away End". This is his first book.

You can visit the website at www.theawayend.net, and follow on twitter @theawayend or on Andrew's personal twitter @a_southwick.

Acknowledgements

Thank you to everyone who contributed to the book, especially to those brave enough to share your stories.

To Ashley Johnston, for the beautiful cover design.

Elizabeth McLaughlin, for rescuing me from the scrapheap and making me a graduate with a CV to be proud of.

To mum, dad and Karen, for bailing me out of trouble so many times.

Preface

Some people live life without regrets. Or at least they say they do. In reality, they've read a quote someone has shared on Facebook, have liked it (in both senses of the word) and decided that will be their new motto.

Of course we have regrets. I have regrets every day. For example I wished I'd woken up an hour earlier this morning, and I wish I'd cooked breakfast rather than reheating the pizza from last night and absorbing the taste of cardboard.

I certainly don't regret going to university. I don't regret not completing the course and switching universities because of what it led to.

However there are a lot of mistakes I wish I hadn't made, and maybe reading a student bible before starting would have helped me do things better than I did.

Except, there wasn't a book written for me. I hadn't written it yet.

There are university guides that tell you to study hard, register for a doctor, and make sure you're well stocked up on pens. There are those that go a little further; telling you to get a store card from Tesco, rent books from the library instead of buying them, join a sports club, or even "How to go food shopping."

All good stuff, except that it doesn't take you four years to work out these things. It takes you a few weeks.

When I was about to start university I was desperate for information. I didn't want to know how to food shop, I wanted to know if I was going to survive university.

I needed to know what living in halls would actually be like. What happens in freshers week? What life would be like for a 23 year old mature student like myself. Am I going to make friends? How do I make friends? How can people hate school but love being a student on a four year degree?

I wanted someone who had done it all to sit down and reveal everything to me, telling me what they regretted doing and if they were in my shoes and getting to do it all again, how they'd do it second time around.

I've written this book not just for the 23 year old me. I've written it for the terrified 17 year old who is about to leave home. I'm writing it for the 40 year old married mature student who is bravely taking the plunge.

It's a guide with all the practical advice any potential student needs, but it's a story first and foremost.

It's the story of how I tried to avoid going to university, eventually went, failed, recovered, went to a different university, and finally got the degree.

It's the story of how I made wrong choices, benefited from them, fell in love, and nearly got stabbed when a drug fuelled flatmate went on the rampage.

It's not just my story though. It's the story of Craig who lived with the flatmate who left the toilet blocked for three months. Emma who got threatened and was nearly beaten up on her first night in halls. Danny who put a holiday before university and found himself off the course.

Those that loved university and those that hated it.

It's how to make the right choices on the UCAS form, how to pass the interview (I've been on both sides having now worked at university).

It's what you must do on your first weekend, your first week, your first six months.

Choosing your flatmates, getting the right job, joining the best clubs, increasing your social circle.

How to actually pass the exams, how to make a class presentation, and what to do if you find you have failed.

It's not a boring checklist, it's the bible on how to ensure your years as a student are the best years of your life. It's how to make sure you graduate, and where the only regret that keeps you awake at night is that it all flew by too quickly.

Introduction

I vividly remember the last time I sat down with my school careers advisor.

There we were, squeezed in against the wall of a long, thin office, not much bigger than your average cupboard. The smell of tippex and hairspray near enough bludgeoning me to death. The whole place seemed to be an afterthought that the school had somehow found space for. No doubt a parent had one day suggested having an area of the school for pupils to discuss what to actually do with their qualifications may not be the worst idea in the world.

Mrs Curly Hair bleakly looked at my very light and feeble looking CV, the pair of us gloomily trying to plan my life and career.

In our previous meeting I'd said I wanted to be a journalist. Since then, a chance conversation with a girl who was studying journalism at college steered me elsewhere, towards a path that fate perhaps had laid out for me.

Why I chose that moment to start listening to women is anyone's guess. The moment of rare courtesy on my part may well have led to a possible misplaced piece of advice, with "avoid it at all costs" from the college student resonating round my head.

My tired careers teacher wearily rubbed her eye and asked: "So, have you thought any more about journalism?"

I had changed my mind. I had changed it from wanting a career in journalism, to having no idea what I wanted at all.

I was 16, hated school, and the thought of going to college to study and extend education wasn't something I was cheerfully looking forward to. That was just college; the thought of university brought up images of long dark corridors, books stacked from floor to ceiling, huge lecture theatres where a man in a tailcoat and top hat drew baffling equations on a large chalkboard, and a world of libraries, classes, homework and privileged posh kids taking over my life.

I had no drive. My only goal in life was going to the football with my mates on a Saturday, heading to the back of what used to be the Beach End at Pittodrie. From there we watched Aberdeen do anything but actually play football, but we somehow found enjoyment from it because it was a release from the boring jobs we had, and about the only thing in my life that I actually cared for.

Away days were light relief too. Early mornings on to the back of the supporters bus, incoherently drunk on makeshift vodka and Irn Bru mixers. A result every week was just making it to the game without getting thrown off the bus or turned away at the turnstiles.

All this was funded by working as a kitchen porter, which is one of those jobs that should give you the urge to better your life. Hard labour, sweaty kitchens, angry chefs, and going home covered in an assortment of left over food. It was actually a good thing looking back – it gave me a work ethic that stands me in good stead today, but back then for me it was nothing more than easy money.

I had no responsibilities, and with money in my pocket I could go out and do what I wanted. Why would I want to ruin it all by spending four years skint, studying day and night at university, surrounded by snotty geeks who preferred science to girls? Plus a tailcoat wouldn't suit me.

So there I was, sat opposite my careers advisor, staring in amazement at her big twirling mass of unkempt tresses, wondering how long she was going to keep the pretence up that she actually cared what I did with my life. I could have announced there and then I was going to become a hitman, assassinating governments for pocket money to fuel my need for fruit machines, fags and kebabs. She probably would have suggested I try get some work experience somewhere in the field.

"Have you anyone you'd like to start your murder spree with dear?"

"Yes, your hairdresser."

I had no clear plan. All I knew was that I couldn't stomach another year of school. Of 9am starts. Of algebra, of "The Catcher in the Rye", the Treaty of Versailles, or "Guten tag, Ich heiße Andrew."

So, with seven Scottish Standard Grades and a single Scottish Higher in History, I swerved sixth year at school and signed up for an Electronic and Electrical engineering course. Mrs Curly Hair was adamant it was worthwhile, and driven by the fact it sounded more a practical course, and I'd always enjoyed Friday afternoons in the completely useless Technological Studies, I signed up.

Half way through my college course, despite a rather apathetic approach, I managed to bag an interview for - believe it or not - a job that specifically wanted people interested in electronic and electrical engineering. They even planned to send the recruit who got the role to do the same course I was already on, so reading my application form they must have been over the moon.

The interview (and tour of the workshop) lasted an hour, most of which I spent yawning. I did a grand job of puncturing any enthusiasm they had for me. I was such a disorganised teenage mess that I had not even thought to change my personal statement on my CV, and so had to endure one of the interviewers reading aloud the part where I said my interest was journalism and I wasn't interested in practical activities, especially anything technical.

I left hoping I wouldn't be offered the job, and to save me wasting anyone else's time I just stopped turning up for the course.

I upgraded from kitchen porter to barman, did a stint as a day porter in a hotel, and then went back to barman. They weren't particularly enjoyable jobs.

The days swayed from trying to keep myself awake in an empty bar, with golf on the TV to satisfy the sole afternoon drinker, to hard graft where I was probably working harder than my pay packet suggested I should have. That meagre pay packet though let me enjoy my football, my nights out chasing girls, my own car so I could chase them a little easier, and if I'd had any sense of style back then I might have spent more money on clothes and a decent haircut rather than the Damon Albarn look I was going for.

By the time I was 21 I had grown up a bit, and realised this couldn't be my life. The love of journalism hadn't left me, so while some might spend their holidays lying on a beach, I actually took a two week break from my day job to do a fortnight's work experience at the local paper as a sports writer.

I loved it, and realised what I'd been missing for the past few years. I stuck at it, spent my Sunday mornings shivering in the cold watching 22 fat hungover blokes attempt to stay upright while kicking a ball about. Eventually, after six months of sending in free match reports, I impressed the sports editor enough to be given paid work covering slightly fitter, but still fat, hungover blokes kicking a ball about.

I was a barman by day, and usually twice I week I was a sports journalist; covering matches, doing interviews, getting full pages to myself in the paper and convincing myself and others I was quite important.

By 22 some people my age were graduating and settling into

highly paid jobs. Most of my old schoolmates were earning big money in the oil industry in the north-east. I told the customers who I was serving pints to I wouldn't be far behind them. I had my journalism job and that would turn into a full-time job one day.

Then I started seeing a rather well-to-do girl who was about to start university. "Why aren't you at university" came the probing question one day in that rather plum accent, as she – perhaps egged on by her mother - weighed up the chances of a long term future for the pair of us. Six years on from school and still nothing had changed; I couldn't be bothered extending my school days.

You see, no-one had actually explained to me what university was really like.

Then I met another three girls over the course of the year. They were all getting ready to start university too. One was staying in Aberdeen, the other two moving to Glasgow and Edinburgh respectively, which I thought was a mad idea. I still was unmoved, even more so when I heard to my horror their courses last at least three years, generally four if they did honours. Why were two of them moving away – four years is a long time to have no mates is it not?

It was inevitable that football would somehow be involved in a life changing decision. It came the weekend of 14th/15th November, 2003.

I had two tickets for Scotland v Holland, the Euro 2004 play-off first leg at Hampden. My friend Laurann was one of the girls who had made the crazy decision to up sticks, don the old Victorian garb, and parade up and down the corridors at Glasgow University. I thought - rather cheekily - if I gave her the spare ticket I not only got to catch up with my pal, I got a floor to sleep on the night before the game.

Now Scotland won 1-0; James McFadden playing a delicious one-two with Darren Fletcher and firing a deflected shot into the back of the net. Hampden Park bounced in ecstasy, and for a few days we dreamed we were heading to Portugal for the European Championships.

That dream died rather cruelly days later with a 6-0 thumping in the second leg. I can still remember watching the game in a nightclub full to the brim of partying Scotsmen and women getting ready to take the roof off, and seeing everyone's hearts slowly punctured as each goal went in. I mean, 6-0? Come on.

However, it still started a journey. I always remember on my drive home back to Aberdeen from Glasgow, all I could think about was Laurann. I'd fallen in love.

No, not with Laurann - as lovely as she may be - but with her new life.

There she was living in a dingy halls of residence. She had to share her room with another girl. There was a huge yellow stain on the carpet. They had a sink, a small desk, two small wardrobes, and that was their room for the year.

To go to the toilet or showers they had to traipse down the corridor and share with everyone else on their floor. They had a choice of three showers – one rarely had hot water and another didn't have much power in it. The popular choice had hair overflowing from the drain where you either took one for the team and picked it up, or straddled the pile and showered while trying to avoid everyone's greasy locks.

Everyone had a key for different kitchens which they shared with up to a dozen others. They had no TV and so walked down to the common room where most of the guys had a nightly Fifa tournament going on the Playstation. Handy for the lads, not so much for any Hollyoaks fans.

However, it looked brilliant. I had never seen Laurann so happy. Granted, I'd only known her for less than a year before she left, but everyone seemed to know her; she had friends behind every door and every corner she walked. The security guards didn't mind the noise, and everyone partied when they wanted and for as long as they wanted. They went clubbing when they felt like it. Even cooking with their mates looked like fun, watching them mix peanut butter and milk to make a sauce for their chicken because they couldn't afford to buy one.

And university? Was it like school? She showed me her timetable, she was hardly ever there. She had classes she had to go to, and classes where she could go if she wanted but no-one would check.

Hold on a second. What the hell had I been doing for the past six years?

I went home, to my house that I shared with my mum and dad. I went back to work to the same boring job, with the same customers asking the same questions. I lived in the same town, five miles from

Aberdeen, where there was no clubs, no bars open after midnight, and very little nightlife to speak of.

All of a sudden, life seemed very boring.

I could stay here, keep doing my £10 an article journalism, hoping one day someone would leave the paper and I'd be offered a full-time job. Or, I could head for another city, move into halls, make new friends, and do what I should have done when I was 18. And I would have to do it now, because if I waited five years and regretted it, then starting uni when I was reaching 30 was going to be a lot less fun than doing it when I was still young enough (and looked young enough) to hang around and party with freshers.

So, university it was then. How hard can it be to bag a place on one of them degrees?

To my dismay, even when considered a mature student, I had nowhere near the qualifications needed to get to university. Even the low level universities and the most basic of courses wanted more than one Higher. It dawned on me I might have to go back to school at the age of 22 to get the necessary qualifications, before thankfully realising you can actually sit them at college.

So I enrolled at the same college I'd made a fairly tame effort at attending in the past, and studied the Highers I thought I'd managed to avoid when I'd left school early.

It was hard. It was a long year surrounded by irritating 15 year olds. We weren't all that annoying at that age were we? At 22 I wasn't used to hearing the teacher stop to tell unruly children to be quiet.

I was also doing it while still working the same boring bar job, living at home when I wanted to be away, and trying to keep a girlfriend happy who was like an angry dominatrix.

I got through it. Got my Highers, and after an interview and test bagged myself a place on BA (Hons) Journalism at Glasgow Caledonian University.

It was, so I was told, the best journalism course in Scotland. On day one of the course they told us we were the elite. Just under 500 people had applied, 100 had been interviewed, and only around 20 of us had been chosen for the course. Apart from a rather sublime piece of finishing in a 9-2 defeat for my football team while at school, and a second place finish in a drawing contest that won me £5, my list of achievements wasn't an extensive list, so this was by far my biggest accolade to date.

Starting September 2005, I was going to be a university student.

However, the degree and actually passing it was secondary to everything. By the time I finally packed my bags and flew the nest, I was 23. I was leaving Aberdeen, or more specifically Westhill, and heading three hours down the road to live in the city centre of Glasgow. I was leaving the house I had lived in since the age of five, and moving in with five strangers whose age, sex and level of drug addiction I knew nothing about.

I remember the excitement. Who would these flatmates be? What would that first day and night actually be like? Would I be walking into an all welcoming flat alongside my new five best friends for life, or would I be regretting everything within 24 hours and crying on the phone to my mother?

What actually is freshers week? What happens? What should I do? Am I going to make friends? What if I don't make friends? I'm 23 while everyone else is 17 or 18, so what am I going to do if everyone avoids me because I'm too old? What if the halls have put me with all the other older students and I'm stuck with people with no interest in embracing the uni life and we're all in bed by 10pm?

Am I going to enjoy the course? I hated school, I wasn't a huge fan of college, what is university going to be like?

Will I survive living on my own in Glasgow? I'm going to get four years of sheepshagging jokes from a bunch of wise cracking weegies. I'm old, I talk different from everyone down there, and my football team is crap so I can forget having any bragging rights over anything.

I was nervous. I was bloody excited too. I daydreamed constantly about it. Even in these times of the internet I was struggling to get information. I wanted to know who my flatmates were, who my course mates were, what I should be bringing, what everyone else would be bringing, and whether I was making the best or worst decision of my life by going there.

Eight years on, I'm writing this book, sat in my Glasgow flat that I bought less than a year ago. My CV has grown a fair bit, and I can boast references from the BBC, the Scottish Football Association, and one of my old lecturers - who later became my boss - at a different university than I first started at in 2005.

I'm taking breaks from writing this guide to go on Facebook and try and organise that university reunion with eight friends I met in Glasgow, but who are now parked from Inverness to Banbridge to

London.

Life has taken a funny turn. When I was 23 and away to start university, never mind when I was 16 and away to leave school, I could never have imagined this was how my life would turn out.

However, university is a journey, and it's likely to be the greatest journey you ever go on.

You **will** make friends, so you can end that worry right away. The only possible way you won't have any mates will be because you've decided to avoid all human contact (and you'll be surprised at how many people actually do) and locked yourself in your bedroom for four years. Do that and you'll succeed in passing your course but miss out on all the fun.

You will have good days and bad. You'll have the best days of your life, but then lie wide awake worrying about money, the essay, the exam, the presentation, that girl/boy you fancy, and about where you're going to live next year and with whom.

You will have regrets. Plenty of them. You'll learn from them and probably laugh about them one day and realise you don't actually regret them at all. It's all part of growing up, and you're going to do a hell of a lot of it over the next four years.

I can't revisit that 23 year old and give him this book. I wish I could, but then again I needed to make some mistakes in order to be able to write this book in the first place. Others still rankle. I wish I could get a hold of the 16 year old and kick some sense into him. I would start by handing him some hair gel.

However, I can give the book to you. Whether you're thinking of going to university, are in the middle of applying, or have your results in the bag and are away to start, then this is the bible for you.

In this book is everything I wished I'd known before I started at university. In addition, I've questioned friends, and in some cases friends have questioned their friends, and given you their stories and advice too.

So you don't just get the story of the 23 year old male studying journalism in Glasgow. You have the girls and boys who went to Aberdeen, Edinburgh and Belfast. Those that loved it, those that hated it, and those that went against every rule in this book.

We can give you an idea of what it'll be like. Hopefully, we'll whet your appetite for it and have you even more excited than you already are.

If you're just thinking about going, then I'll try to help you make the correct choices on your UCAS form.

If you've got interviews to attend, then I'm the perfect man to help, because I've seen them from both sides. I've had to do an interview to get on the course, and I've sat on the other side helping to interview potential students. I've got all the inside secrets.

In chapters three and four I'll make sure you've got everything sorted for that first day, then take your hand and lead you into halls and tell you what everything is really going to be like, along with the tips and hints and the things you **must** do on that first weekend that could set you up for the rest of your time at university.

I've experienced pretty much every type of flatmate there is to have; from the shy to the eccentric, from the batty to the dangerous. I'll help you survive and help you make the right decisions when it comes to picking your flatmates and accommodation for second year.

I'll help you with getting the right job while at university, and joining the right clubs to ensure your social circle continues to grow while you're a student.

There's advice if you're a young, shy teenager who's not good at making friends, and there's advice for the mature student returning to study after years away from education.

And within it all, I'll also help you handle the degree, and any expected bumps along the way.

At the end of the day, nothing in this book is going to spoil your enjoyment. I can't spoil the surprise because university life is unique to every person.

You're going to love it. I'm just going to help you love it a little bit more.

1
What University to go to

We may as well get some boring stuff out of the way.

It's all well and good getting ready for a four year party. However if you're not happy with the course or institution you're at, you'll be the one in the corner texting your parents for a lift home before the festivities have got into full swing.

Firstly, get yourself every prospectus you can get your hands on. Some of the websites are poor and don't do the university justice – get a proper prospectus to look at. Take one to bed every night and take the time to read through them properly. You may find yourself being attracted to a career you never even knew existed.

All through your school life you may never have considered working in communications, forensics or occupational therapy. You may never have heard of courses such as mechatronics, parasitology or virology.

It's not a bad idea to plan your life out. Think of the degree and what use it'll do for you, maybe even look at what postgraduate courses that would open the door to, and see what job opportunities it could create.

Do you want to go on a year long placement in a different city? Some courses offer that, so start considering that and weighing up if it's something you could afford to do.

It's something that's overlooked by most people who generally are choosing a university simply because their friends are going or because they want to move to that particular city

University Tours

University tours are designed to help the student have a "feel" for the place, a stroll through the surrounding areas, and make an informed decision over which institution to spend the next three/four years of their lives studying at.

If you are moving to a different town or city, then you won't be able to really find out what living in that area of the country is like until you are there for at least a few weeks, and sometimes it takes a few months for you to properly settle in a new place if you've been used to the same town all your life.

It will take more than a few hours to find out what the people are like, the best shops, the trendiest bars, which morning sandwich shop is likely to give the best student discounts, that brilliant little pizza place that gives you free toppings because they know you're a regular, that little known nightclub hidden in a side street where the bouncers let you skip the queue, where is best to get that spray tan, and all the other little things that are perhaps important to you and are likely to become part of your life while you are a student.

However, sometimes you do step in a place and it just feels right. A gut instinct if you will. And therefore paying a visit isn't a bad idea if it's something you can do with little hassle. However, I wouldn't advocate booking flights and pricing up hotels just to take in an open day.

> **TIP:** *Try and learn a new language while at university. It's something extra to have on the CV and increases your job options.*
>
> *Some foreign students will teach the language to earn a bit of extra money, and at a much lower cost than normal lessons.*
>
> *I'm now learning Spanish but wish I'd done it when I had a Spanish flatmate in first year to help me.*

Open days can be handy if you're moving to a small town where you're worried there won't be much to do. Perhaps you have been told some horror stories about a place and wish to investigate yourself to put your mind at rest.

However, don't expect to find all the answers about a town, city or even country based on one visit.

If you are going to an open day though, make the most of it.

A university tour is worthwhile if interested in knowing the facilities and what the accommodation actually looks like. If you have two or more offers, then chances are the tour will help you make up your mind.

If you can get speaking to a current student, then great. Make sure you ask what the course is really like.

Students are generally quite honest, they have no hidden agenda so they won't tell you it's great to get you on the course if they know it's not.

What you want to be asking about the course is how much of your chosen subject you actually get to do.

For example at Glasgow Caledonian only a third of the coursework in first and second year seemed to be journalism.

At the University of the West of Scotland, where I would later end up studying, I would say it was more like 75%.

That doesn't mean one course is better than the other.

At Caley they were concentrating on giving you the best possible degree so there were a lot of other subjects as part of the course.

At UWS, it was more vocational, and although there was still non-journalism modules on the timetable, it was more centered on turning you into a journalist.

What people rarely pay attention to, and it was something I didn't even realise until I started the course, was the "school" that your degree is based in.

Universities have different schools – business school, arts and creative school, health, computing, and so on. Where your degree is based will determine what other modules you will be doing.

I presumed all journalism courses were the same, but at Glasgow Caley it was in the business school. At other universities it tends to be their art and creative industries school, so a lot of the modules and way of teaching were different.

Read the prospectus carefully and look closely at what list of modules you're actually being given.

There's no right or wrong answer about which one to do. I couldn't actually recommend to you which of the two courses I studied on was better. It's simply down to you and where you want your career to go. Believe it or not, not everyone who signs up to a journalism course wants to be a journalist so the actual degree might be more important.

I did two years of journalism at Caley, and went directly into third year of sports journalism at UWS. For me that was perfect as I got the best of both worlds, even though doing two courses wasn't my initial plan.

I don't regret not doing the whole degree at Caley and I wouldn't have wanted to start from first year at UWS either.

> ***TIP:*** *Sign up to all the reward cards at supermarkets. You will never go a week without needing to do some shopping, so you may as well earn points while you're there and get sent gift vouchers in return. You can double your points by saving and re-using your old bags.*
>
> *Many will give you receipts with things like "£6 off when you spend over £40". There's no need to spend £40 of your money – get the flatmates to chip in and buy some communal things like toilet roll and bin bags to get the price up. Then make sure you pocket the discount and the points on your store card!*
>
> *Note –* ***don't*** *sign up for in store credit cards. Your student loan isn't enough to cover them.*

You can't find out the real answers to your questions in a prospectus or by speaking to any of the tutors. You find that out by speaking to the students. If you can't find someone at an open day, then go on Facebook, search for a current student at your chosen university doing your course, and just send them a message asking if they mind answering a few questions about it.

Ask about work experience too. Some places will leave it up to you to find your own work experience, others will have good contacts already established. Ask if they have guest lecturers, they could be well known people from the industry.

Don't be shy to ask if the course is worth it. They might tell you they're hoping to transfer to another course or uni, or they might tell you about how their mate is at another university and he/she thinks their course is better/worse.

Of course, take everything with a pinch of salt. It is worth a lot as it is coming from experience, but do your own investigating and make sure it's you deciding whether to go or not, and not someone you knew for five minutes. Remember the girl who talked me out of a journalism course when I was 16? I'll never know if she was right.

> ***TIP:*** *Bring a plug extension on day one. You will need it. Also collect your empty Chinese takeaway tupperware boxes, they are useful for when you want to buy meat or fish in bulk. Then you can separate them into tubs and freeze them, saving you money in the long run.*

I'm going to touch on accommodation and facilities below, but ask the students about them.

Ask what the halls are like, is the security good (that means many things – is the place safe for starters, but are they also easy going; do they let you enjoy yourselves), are the rooms clean, what is the area they live in like (not all halls of residence are on or near campus), do the halls have free Wifi?

Ask about the facilities – how easy is it to get books from the library, how easy is it to get on a computer, and what are the opening hours.

> *TIP: You don't need to have a medicine cabinet that would make a doctor proud. However, have a packet of Lemsip cold and flu tablets (or similar brand) at your bedside, plus a stash of easy-on-the-nose tissues. They're a godsend when you wake up with the flu, saving you having to make the trek in the snow to get some. Remember your mum won't be knocking on your door with a bowl of soup when you're ill.*

The University Library

Sounds boring, I mean what a place to start - the library. Chances are, you barely stepped foot in your school library the entire time you were there. A public library was probably something alien to you. And here you are being told to put your university's library at the height of importance.

Here's the thing. At university, you will spend just as much time in your library as you do sleeping. You may even combine the two.

At Glasgow Caledonian, the library was actually being built when I started; the rather impressive Saltire Centre as it became to be known. One semester in and it opened, complete with four floors of books, computers, printers and photocopiers.

It had couches designed for group work. What use does sitting round a table do, we all do our best thinking when lying on our backs. Insert your own dirty joke here.

The basement and first floor you could work and chat like a normal, sociable student should. Second floor was the quiet floor, handy for them days when you needed to knuckle down and get something finished off. And, in the odd chance you didn't get the message, the third floor was the silent floor. As I grew to learn, quiet meant you were allowed a couple of coughs at best, any more than two and you were being rowdy. Silent though meant breathe at your peril, the death stare from others was always waiting.

The library, whether you like it or not, will become your second home. Trying to get a computer any time after 9am, no matter how many computers your university may possess, is akin to getting a date with a supermodel. Unless you are a supermodel, in which case it's akin to getting a date with me. Oh aye, I'm just warming up.

So, you wait until after 4pm when people start to drift home, and you grab your computer then. And that 3,000 word essay that needs to be done keeps you there until you are eventually thrown out at 11pm.

That was Glasgow Caledonian University though. The West of Scotland University was much smaller – Hamilton campus at least. Change the 11pm closing time to 6pm. Change four floors to one. Change 300 computers to a dozen. Even reduce your £15 yearly printing credits to a fiver.

The smaller the library, the less books that are available. And you will need to read a lot of books, because you will be marked down big time for failing to do any background reading or referencing properly. More of actually passing your course later though.

The University of West of Scotland in fairness was split into four campuses; Paisley, Hamilton, Ayr and Dumfries. So the small library was acceptable due to the fact you could order a book through your library from a different campus and have it sent to your place of worship for you. Sounds great, but if you're writing your essay at the last minute then that is no help to you, so you need to be more organised if your campus facilities aren't set-up for the student who leaves their coursework to the last hour.

If you can find a library that opens late on weekends then you're on to a winner. Glasgow Caledonian did open on Saturday and Sunday which was pretty decent, but closed at 6pm both days. It always annoyed me that, as Sunday night appeared the best time to actually be in there. Nothing was on TV, flatmates had gone home for the weekend or were working weekend jobs, the nights students tend to go out drinking is midweek – it was the one evening I actually had the desire to go and do some work.

It should be noted though, a lot of universities will open 24 hours a day over the exam period. Yes, you could actually be sat at your computer at 4am studying away. It wasn't uncommon to go on a night out, be clubbing with your mates until 3am, scoff a kebab, stumble towards the library, buy yourself a coffee to attempt to sober up (or even better just take out the hip flask and keep going Oliver Reed style), and get cracking on an essay.

- Quick sum up.

Check out the library, paying particular attention to the number of computers it has, and weigh it up with the number of students who go there. If you have 50 computers in a university with 30,000 students, you're going to have a problem. It won't be such a major problem if it is open late though when the university is quiet.

Ask about opening times, and think about when you're likely to be studying. If you're working or planning to go home at weekends, then the library being shut on a Saturday or Sunday won't effect you. All boring stuff but at the end of the day you're there to get a degree.

TIP: You will rarely have as much spare time after your student years are over, therefore use yours wisely. Do as much as you can when not in class, working and studying.

Accommodation

The thing with university accommodation is that on a tour it will probably look lovely, shiny and tidy. The universities generally pick an empty flat, or one that they know is kept clean by its residents, and let you see it in its best days. In reality, your accommodation will never be truly clean.

You have to remember here you could be sharing with maybe seven fellow students, more than likely all teenagers, and in most cases all living away from home for the first time.

Dishes will pile up, bins will overflow, and carpets will stain. People will spill milk in the fridge and leave it for months until it creates a smell that entrances the whole flat. Memories from that legendary party you held will linger for a long time.

You won't find out who your flatmates are on the university tour, unless by some miracle you happen to meet someone on it and arrange there and then to live with each other. Don't bank on that happening though.

Every accommodation is different. One university might offer exceptionally large bedrooms, and I've seen some with huge balconies for you to enjoy in summer.

In general though, expect rooms to be small and basic.

If they are en-suite, the showers will probably flood. You may even struggle to get hot water at 8.30am as you find you're using your shower at the same time as everyone else in your block.

You might get lucky with a view; my bedroom looked straight onto a brick wall and the living room/kitchen looked on to a motorway.

Check out the accommodation simply if you have a choice of where to stay. By that, I mean the larger universities will offer different types of halls in different locations, from luxury flats to dingy dormitories.

You'll find some are right on campus, others a walk or even a bus ride away.

Some might be in a good area of town, others you might not want to be walking home by yourself late at night to.

The choice you get to make might simply be between en-suite and non en-suite.

Here's one choice I am hereby not allowing you to make. Promise me one thing new student.

You will, whatever the state of your halls, no matter the fear of living with flatmates riddled with lice, you must not waver from the oath you are now about to take.

If there is one thing I will write in this book that is the height of importance, then it is this.

You MUST, without doubt, without giving it a second thought, spend your first year in the official halls of residence.

It's not even up for debate. No ifs or buts.

No "My dad is buying me a penthouse in the city centre where I'm flat sharing with Michelle Keegan."

You move into university halls or you don't bother going to university at all.

Okay that's a bit harsh, but trust me, it will be something you will regret if you don't give it just one year in halls.

Michelle Keegan would make a rubbish flatmate anyway, I'll tell you why later in the book.

Half the experience of being a student - perhaps the greatest experience - is cutting your ties and moving out for the first time, and what better way to do it than in halls where every flat is full of your mates?

If you are attending a university in your own city, then you'll find it hard to get rewarded a place in halls on account outside students get priority. But, you can at least apply.

Even if you are at first rejected, ask to be put on a waiting list as some students do leave after a few weeks due to homesickness and spaces become available.

You can apply to live in private halls of course, and you generally won't have as much trouble being accepted there. However, private halls would be your second choice, ideally you want to be in the official halls.

It's not about the actual accommodation itself – many private halls are cheaper and come with better facilities.

It's about the social life and the unforgettable experience of starting your new life alongside hundreds of other freshers in the same boat as you, and going on that same three or four year journey with strangers who will go on to be some of the best friends you ever have.

Private halls are not all first years, or even people attending the same university as you. They are a mix, so it's not quite the same.

The experience of moving in on the same day as all the friendless freshers isn't there either, and you don't meet as many pals.

A few of us stayed in private halls in second year, and we were pro-active enough to throw a party that first night for everyone in our block, went knocking on some doors, and did meet some good friends that we stuck with throughout the year, but it was still nowhere on the same scale as first year.

Everyone I spoke to who didn't choose to live in halls now regrets it. They maybe had no desire to do it at the time, but they all look back and realise they made a mistake.

Please, if you only take one bit of advice from this book, move into halls.

I never stayed in halls because I didn't see the point. I only lived half an hour from uni, had a part time job at home, my boyfriend lived close by, I had no bills to pay, clothes to wash, a bed to make or food to pay for and cook. Why would I even think about moving into halls?

Living with strangers, surviving on toast, freezing my tits off in a cold, weak shower and stuck in a tiny bedroom with only a messy kitchen to share? Sounds like a prison sentence to me.

What if you didn't get on with the people you were staying with? What if you got on with the people you were staying with a little bit too much?

Could you blame me for sticking to my home comforts? Halls? More like hells. But what I didn't see, though, were the things beyond that and I only began to notice them when I started visiting my new friends in their halls.

The rooms weren't cold and impersonal, they were decorated with film posters, shelves were cluttered with frames full of happy photos, and friends huddled under blankets to watch crap TV on, well, crap TVs. The unwashed dishes were glasses from the previous night's party, and the flat mates were interesting people from all over the world looking to have an adventure just like you.

Halls don't have to be prison cells, they can be your first home away from home. So if you're in two minds whether to move or not, think about it this way – do you want to wake up ten minutes before your lecture and still make it on time? Do you want to live a stones throw from all the best bars and clubs? Do you want to share your uni experience with other young, excited and nervous people just like yourself?

Take it from me – a 25 year old who has only just left home and moved into her first flat – if I could go back seven years and do this again I would have moved out when uni laid the chance on a plate for me.

The sense of independence and adventure which comes with starting that new chapter in your life is priceless, and if ever there was a time to be doing it, it's at the start of university – the best years of your life.

Laura Brannan

At Glasgow Caledonian our halls consisted of flats, and in fact we had a choice; en-suite and non en-suite (or "the ghetto" as they were dubbed).

En-suite consisted of flats of six. Generally, though there were exceptions, these were split to have three girls and three boys, with at least one of these students a foreigner.

Some places don't like that idea and will only have flats of all boys and all girls. It's a silly idea, you're not going to keep the opposite sex apart and you're certainly not going to stop them having sex in halls either.

If it is something you feel strongly about for whatever reason though you can usually request an all-girl or all-boy flat. However try and go for a mixed flat – you don't want to fancy any of your flatmates (we'll touch on living with Michelle Keegan later), but you do want to fancy one of their mates and have your flatmate set you up. (None of mine did come to think of it. One of my flatmates was friends with strippers and she still never set me up. Another had a hot Aberdonian as a mate who was doing nursing, but no I was still never set up. Thanks girls if you're reading. It's fine, I'm away to slate you both in another chapter anyway).

> **NOTE:** *Your halls will usually be rented out as cheap hotel rooms during summer. It's not uncommon to find some halls even rent them out during the university timetable. One particular halls of residence are known to kick their students out for four weeks to rent elsewhere. Remember to check the small print for any unexpected surprises.*

I took the en-suite choice, because I liked the thought of being able to go to the toilet and take a shower at any time of day or night that I wanted, without having to wander down a corridor drunk in the dark. I also like the thought of knowing that if I clean a bathroom it's going to still be clean when I get back to it, and I'm not spending my time cleaning up someone else's dirt. (if my current flatmate is reading this, you might want to take that as a hint.)

However, the ghetto was much cheaper, and were usually bigger flats. A friend had the unusual situation of being the only boy in a flat of eight. He thought he was in a dream straight away before the struggle began to get in the shower. Having two showers in a flat that consists of seven teenage girls causes very obvious problems.

I saw some of Edinburgh University's halls when I visited a rather plush complex known as Holland House. In there (or at least the block I was in) you don't actually have flatmates, and in fact lived in a sort of dormitory with a key to your room that housed a shower and toilet (and a balcony, which was rather pleasant. It also came in handy for a neighbour who used it for a suicide attempt. Not everyone enjoys university I suppose..).

No flatmates, but you do have a shared kitchen that you and several others have keys for, so the opportunity was still there to make friends fast, but I would say most people prefer an actual flat.

The aforementioned Laurann was staying in the cheapest accommodation Glasgow University had, and with 30,000 students they had a lot to choose from. So cheap in fact that she did not even have the room to herself.

I'll let her tell the story...

"I lived in Cairncross Halls in Glasgow. It is a classic 'halls' in that none of the accommodation was self-contained flats but rather floors of bedroom doors and several shared kitchens. Most residents had to share a room.

"Sharing a room with a stranger could have had its difficulties but I was sharing with a friend from school (arranged beforehand) so I already had a friend."

Maybe I'm pampered but I could put up with that for a few weeks – but not for months on end. However, we're all different, and the location was actually superb as it was right on the door step of the trendy west end and all its bars and cafes.

We can ponder all day as to the merits of accommodation, but we're missing the important facts here. What your halls really look like are not important, because first year will fly by. And when you move out, cursing how quickly the year has gone, you won't miss your room or flat for it's furniture or facilities. You will miss it because you got to spend nine months living in the same building as all your best friends.

You will realise very quickly in second year that your new flat may be much better than halls. You may have better comforts, a much bigger room, you might even have better flatmates because you got to choose them this time, and you may be in a far better location and paying much less for the privilege. But having all your 20/50/100 new mates spread across the city is not nearly as much fun as being able to nip down the corridor and go on a hunt for a party or someone to go clubbing with you.

Now you're saying goodbye at the taxi rank to your mates and arranging to meet up next week, when before you drunkenly walked home together stealing traffic cones and hoovers (it was there, I couldn't help it. The policeman who stopped me thought I was an idiot) and continuing the party in halls.

You will never be bored. There will always be someone up for doing something. I lost count of the times I'd go to do my washing or nip out to the supermarket, and come back having been invited on a night out because you'd passed someone's open window and got chatting.

> **TIP:** *When you move in to halls, sign up to an insurance company online and insure everything in your room. You might have a lock for your door but your flat will become a social hub where people you don't know are constantly walking in and out to visit your flatmates. Thefts are very common.*

I give you that advice even if you're a mature student. I was two months shy of turning 24 when I moved in.

Okay, so maybe if you're a lot older than that, well into your 30's or 40's and set in your ways, then you're probably not going to university looking to experience the same social life the younger students will.

However, if you're under the age of 30 then I'd still consider halls, and if you're under the age of 25 then you're definitely still young enough.

I know I wouldn't have missed out on halls for the world, because first year of university will be far better than you ever imagine it to be. Life is about to get really interesting.

2
UCAS and Interviews

This book is designed to let you in on university secrets, so here's secret number one.

Getting into university can sometimes be harder than passing university.

You will be constantly told throughout your Highers (or the equivalent outwith Scotland) that university work far exceeds what you get at school. That is true; the essay standards are far higher and as pointed out in the last chapter you will spend half your time camped in the library.

However you'll find your own standards raise, and simply your own maturity due to the environment you're in, and so it becomes easier to obtain the passes at university than it is at school. Unless of course you're doing a very hard degree, but surely you'll be a very clever young man/lady, in which case don't worry about it champ.

Essentially in first year university just sends a higher volume of work your way than school did. However you have much more free time. At school you were there all day and it felt like the weekends were your release. At university you'll have plenty of days off, and even the days you've got classes it's rare to find yourself in all day.

I struggled more with my Highers than I did with first year of university. Maybe it was because I had gone back to college at the age of 22 to do them, sharing classes with 15 year olds who I found it impossible to bond with on account they were irritating little 15 year olds who should have been at school.

I found my Highers stressful though. I felt like there was more pressure on me, that if I failed I wasn't going to university and I would have wasted a year of my life.

Should be said, if you're considered a mature student, then you usually get a slight concession, which is why I was allowed just three Highers instead of the usual four.

You sit them exams though knowing that if you fail, you can't resit them. You can redo the year and improve your mark, but your university only accepts your first score in each subject, so in reality you need to take a different subject. I didn't fancy taking Highers in Maths or any Science subject in order to get the required grades.

So I felt the pressure all right. I had to really knuckle down and make sure I knew everything I could because failure just wasn't an option, not at 22 (no reason to stress as much if you're only 17 or 18).

On the other hand, university will send plenty of exams, essays and assessments your way. You will even have to stand and give class presentations. However they are all obstacles that you will take in your stride, so don't worry about them, because even if you fail, you have not failed your course.

This is because, and this will differ at each institution or course; you usually will get a second, maybe a third and sometimes even a fourth attempt at passing any failed exam or essay.

You will also find a generous marking system. A 40% pass rate generally does the business and gives you a pass. And 40% of a university essay may as well be as good as 90% on a university essay because in first year your marks mean nothing towards your final grade.

At school though, 40% is unlikely to get you the grade you need to get to university.

Before you've sat your exams of course, you'll have gone through the process of making your choices and filling in the UCAS form.

I went to Art School and gained a BDes in Product Design. Worth it, I think. Hindsight tells me it may not have been the degree that best suited my interests towards the end of the four years (all I want to do is draw). Not necessarily a bad thing!

It was fairly diverse, I managed to learn a new language (a bit), have a stint teaching in Secondary Schools, work with clients such as the NHS, present to Government officials, and the opportunity to study abroad for up to two years. All lovely looking stuff on a CV! I may not have had as varied an education had I chose an illustration course.

Ashley Johnston

UCAS Form

One of my regrets, and something which actually made waiting for the exam results much more stressful, was that I didn't think through my UCAS choices.

One thing I did do before applying was visit the college career's teacher. I already knew I wanted to do journalism, but I wanted to see if this visit to a career's adviser was going to be more beneficial than the visit I made at school.

She'd done her homework, knew what journalism courses were considered the best, who was accredited and who wasn't, and even good courses to take should I not get into journalism (they are famously oversubscribed).

However, she hadn't studied journalism, didn't know any journalists, didn't know what editors were actually looking for, and therefore we both agreed English would be a good course to have as a second choice. In reality, that's a lot of nonsense.

I had a maximum of six choices on my UCAS form, and used all six. Something I shouldn't have done, because I should have left one option open.

I ordered all the prospectuses. I don't think there was a Scottish university whose prospectus I didn't read.

I never had any ambition to live in Dundee, but the prospectus did a great job and sold the place to me, and in fact that I had English at Dundee as one of my choices.

It worked out to be a daft choice. I had not even looked into what studying English involved (got the prospectus and spent more time looking at the pictures of halls than I did the course), but as above I'd figured with journalism courses being competitive, doing English seemed like the logical substitute.

That is until you realise just how different an English and journalism course is.

Not only that, but when UCAS returned the verdict that I had an conditional offer, but that it involved needing AAB, I realised it was a waste of time as I was now looking for an A in Higher English which I was never going to get.

If you're thinking of English I should point out I'm not trying to put you off. I'm trying to put you off if you're wanting to be a journalist. If you can't get into a journalism course, then go for something relevant. For example, take a business course if you want to be a business journalist, politics perhaps if you want to be a political journalist. Then use your degree to get you a post-grad in journalism, while getting as much work experience as possible.

There are many similar examples for your own chosen path. Have a good think about it and at least try and think how your degree is going to be relevant to what you want to do as a career.

I also applied for Aberdeen university, on account that you never know what can happen in a year and I may have needed to stay at home. That was a good idea and you maybe should apply for your home town. Don't apply for the wrong course though – I plumped for English again, though the BBC conditional offer at least was more achievable.

The others were Glasgow Caledonian, Napier, Bell College, and Strathclyde. The first three all BA journalism courses, the latter a rather strange journalism/creative writing course that had to be combined with something else.

Strathclyde, as you can imagine, I hadn't thought through.

Napier I had the rather arrogant feeling that an interview was guaranteed. The nerves started to kick in when I got an early and firm rejection. I've never worked out why I got rejected there but offered an interview at Glasgow Caledonian which is considered a better course. You may find yourself rejected at a uni you're not even that keen on and accepted for your first choice.

I had applied to Bell College on my careers adviser's recommendation. As the name says, it was a college, a small one at that. In addition, it was based in Hamilton, a small town with not much in it. I got offered an interview, but as it got closer I thought more about how I would be moving to a small town, a small campus, and it just didn't seem like it would be a step up from where I already was. So I rejected the offer.

In a quirky twist of fate, that college later became part of the University of the West of Scotland, and I spent a year studying at Hamilton before being employed to work there for a further 18 months. I don't regret not taking that offer though because at the time it would have been the wrong choice and I'm still glad my freshers year was in Glasgow. Again, don't just apply for the course, apply to the town/city you want to be living in.

Glasgow Caledonian was left as the firm first choice now, but things weren't looking good. I'd found out that 500 people had applied, and only 100 were being interviewed, with only 20 of that were being accepted on the course. Interviews had started taking place at the turn of the year, and as the months came and went I hadn't heard a thing.

I'd used up all my UCAS choices, so I couldn't now make a late application to another university, which ruled out the journalism course at Stirling, which I should have had as a choice.

It meant I'd have to wait for clearing, and with the competitive journalism courses all likely to be gone I would have been left doing a course I had no intention of ever doing.

Around April the letter arrived from Glasgow Caledonian and put my fears to rest; *"Interview next week. Please bring some examples of your work."*

Result. The hard part was over. Now the easy part of passing a test and winning over the course leaders.

Union! Union! Union!! You will regret not going often enough in later years. There may well be a cracking DJ line up at a certain club in town, but there will still be cracking line ups in the clubs once you no longer have the union.

Colin Struthers

Interview

I'm strange in that I don't mind interviews. I find sitting in a lecture hall for two hours more worrying than a 15 minute interview. It's shorter, you're talking too much to worry about nerves, and I'm a rubbish listener anyway.

Not everyone needs to attend an interview. Generally, most go by your exam results and UCAS application, but some of the over subscribed courses cut their students down through interviews. There's possibly a double meaning in that.

I arrived early on what was an uncommonly hot day. I sat outside, soaked up the rays, watched all the beautiful women that studied there walk by, and knew I had to get accepted. As I said in chapter one, you sometimes get a gut instinct this is the place for you, and that morning I got it.

Perhaps it's that "getting a feel for the university" thing they talk about. Perhaps it was because I felt this was now my only chance of doing journalism at university, and my only chance of moving to Glasgow which I'd now set my heart on. It may just been that I'm small minded and was impressed by the number of women I saw.

After sitting for a bit and enjoying the sun, I went up and found a tiny little room full of a dozen fellow interviewees. People were arriving at different times due to our different interview spots, but because of what we were told was a backlog we were all there for a couple of hours, with nothing to do but fill in a short test and make no effort whatsoever to talk to each other.

I'd arrived in shirt, tie, trousers and smart shoes. Others were in jeans and trainers, but another guy was in a suit. Was I under dressed or over dressed?

The test was easy enough, just basically a general knowledge quiz about what was happening in the world. As long as you read the papers you knew the answers, though I was later told by someone who made it onto the course that as he filled in his test a girl beside him nudged him and said "Who's the American president?"

The interview wasn't too taxing either. Two important men from the world of media – one time BBC stalwart Ken and a hard nosed ex-newspaper editor Julian fired the questions at me. I just kept to the mantra I had always been told; if you don't like the question you're asked, then answer the question you think you should have been asked.

That my friends is how to get through your university interview. When they ask "Why do you want to be a journalist", you don't answer it literally. Instead, pretend they've asked you "What journalism related things have you spent your life doing" and take the opportunity to boast about the three years worth of work experience you've been up to. You're still giving them their answer – you're just giving them a better answer.

When they ask you what sets you apart from the other candidates, tell them about your greatest achievement, or when you went that extra mile for someone.

What are your strengths? Don't list things like "good listener, hard worker, nice haircut." Tell them good things you've done and explain it to them.

They never asked me how I got my foot in the door at my local paper, but I told them about it anyway, explaining I'd been getting up every Sunday morning to stand at the side of the pitch in order to send in match reports that I never got paid for.

Basically, just talk. Show some passion. Show some understanding for the subject and why the skills you'll learn on the degree will help you. Don't act like you already know everything.

Never give short answers because that's what everyone else is doing. Don't be scared to ramble on. They know you're nervous, they know you're maybe going to get muddled up and stressed. They don't expect an accomplished person to walk in for an interview – but they want someone who can show them they are desperate to do the course, has worked hard to that point and will work hard through-out the course. Sometimes being a bit nervous can be endearing as it shows getting on the course is a big deal to you. Being cocky or trying to be funny won't necessarily impress them.

I've witnessed these university interviews from both sides now, having sat in on the other side of the desk while at UWS, and asked my own questions to potential students. So I'm in a good position to help you through these.

Want tips on exactly what you're asked? It's quite simple; they want to know if you really want to be on that course, or if you just liked what you saw in the prospectus. No-one wants to have to put up with a student changing courses, especially one where it's been so competitive to get in. They don't want to be giving lectures to students who looked bored, they want you showing enthusiasm every week because it makes them feel like their job is worth it.

They also want to see clearly that you have the drive to succeed. You might be going to university because you've heard it's all sex, drugs and student discounts, but they don't want to hear that. Also, what are you like in public? Can they trust you not to embarrass them should they send you on placement?

More importantly, they're weighing you up to see if you can be a journalist, nurse, architect, teacher, or whatever it is you're being interviewed for.

Make sure you have left the interview telling them everything they should know about you. Don't walk out wishing you'd had the opportunity to tell them about something that's not on your CV, but you didn't because they never asked you about it. Slip it into an answer and tell them anyway.

Also make sure you have some questions of your own prepared at the end. You might want to ask about the course more fully, ask about the work experience opportunities, ask if last year's graduates have managed to find jobs, what a typical week in each semester is like. Don't ask how long your holidays are (unless it's because you'll be looking for work experience during that time) or if it's true you don't always have to go to lectures.

The worst thing you can do in an interview is try and get out of it as soon as possible. Giving short answers so you can get it over and done with is the wrong thing to do.

My first night away from home wasn't quite what I expected.

My halls flat was with a group of other girls who all seemed lovely. After having waved my mum off and settled in we decided that we should have a party. Little did I know how it was going to turn out.

Two of the girls had been staying in the halls for quite some time as they were doing some summer classes at the uni. During this time they had met a few local boys and so we invited them along to the party. Later in the night one of these local boys got a little out of hand and started wrecking our kitchen. I either asked him to stop or leave (cant quite remember) to which he pushed me, resulting in another guy stepping in to stick up for me, which then lead to a full scale brawl. There were holes in the wall, lots of blood, and really the most terrifying experience ever for someone spending their first night away from home!

This all came to a head with the police being called and the accommodation officers stepping in. I was absolutely petrified and had my dad come down to get me. The girls in the flat were not giving me much sympathy either as it was their friend.

However later when things calmed down two of the nicer boys I met at the party (Steve and Irish Andy) mentioned that there was still a room in Andy's flat unoccupied, and so myself and my dad asked for me to be moved into their flat, to which they were very accommodating and moved me the next morning....and the rest they say is history!

Emma Rochford

I'll give you some specific examples of questions you may be asked if you're applying to a journalism course. Try and think how this will relate to your interview if it is another subject you're applying for.

You will probably be asked "Where do you get your news from?". Give more than one example. A follow up question after that will be something like "What do you think of their political coverage" or "What journalists do you like to read from that paper?"

The thinking is they're looking for a journalist, so you should have a knowledge and appreciation of journalism. I remember talking about the Scottish Sun's attitude to the Scottish National Party and Labour, and saying it was clear they hadn't yet decided who to back in the next election. It wasn't anything eye opening, I hadn't talked about left wing or right wing policies or talked about their attitude to income tax. I just showed I had been reading the paper, reading their political coverage, and could clearly see what any other reader would. It showed I had an interest in what was happening in the world and was reading about it every day in the paper.

We'd have people come in and say they don't read any papers, and got their "news" from ESPN. That's not even local sport never mind local news. If you've no interest in finding out what's happening in your local town, how are you going to be able to find stories and report on it?

In short, if you want to be a journalist, you don't suddenly take an interest in journalism on day one of the course. That will be the same for marketing, fashion, nursing, art, history, politics, or whatever course it is you're looking to do.

No-one wants you to have a bad interview. Don't be afraid to pause either to think of an answer – you're not racing against the clock, you're allowed to think what you're going to say. Don't pause for too long obviously but don't rush out an answer and then forget what you wanted to say.

Take your time, look the interviewer in the eye, and give as detailed answer as you can give.

I always remember our course leader telling us on the first day of the course at Caledonian that we had all said at least one thing in our interview that had convinced them we could make it as a journalist.

That's true. From sitting on the other side at interviews, it did sometimes only take one big thing to be impressed, and know if that person was a potential student or not. Their first answer might have been impressive and from then on you're willing them to keep up the good answers and net their place. Others, after the first minute you could see they were clueless, and didn't prepare themselves at all for the interview. You wanted to shake them and ask if they realised just because they'd shown up, that hadn't got them on the course.

As long as you've gone in there with something to say, and get it all out before leaving the room, then you've won half the battle.

> ***TIP:*** *If you have to travel to university, whether it's by train or bus, than you might be able to claim travel expenses, even if you are already claiming a student loan. Check with your award agency.*

I'll let you in on a secret. Generally this will be true, but it isn't 100% accurate because there are exceptions, especially if your interviewer isn't actually the one deciding your place on the course.

However, once you leave the room, by the time you've got as far as the lifts your fate has probably already been decided. You're either in the "unconditional", "conditional", or "definitely not" tray. There is the odd one who gets a "I'm not sure about them" and they might need a wee read of anything you've been asked to bring in, but generally the interviewer has made up their mind at the end.

It wasn't even me making the final decision as I was generally just sitting in on interviews and asking the odd question, but I knew if that person had made it on or not because I just had to compare them to everyone else that had been in. It really is that easy to spot a good interview and a bad one.

You have rarely done just okay in an interview. It was either good enough or it wasn't. In a very competitive course you might have a good interview but still be edged out by people that were better than you.

The "Not sure about them" people were actually bad interviews, but may have still showed some promise that had the lecturer thinking. An example of that would be having a good CV but being poor at your interview. The interviewer might be unimpressed at your meeting, but have looked at all your work experience and know you've got potential somewhere.

I don't want to stress you about your interview. I just want you to appreciate the need to talk and have something to say. If you're going to an interview knowing you have a stack of stories and things about yourself to talk about, and have done the minimum research needed for your chosen field, then you don't actually have any reason at all to be nervous.

If you think you've done well, you probably have. After my interview I thought it was actually a bit shorter than everyone else's, but I knew I'd said everything I wanted to say and couldn't think of any question I would have answered differently.

After my interview, four days later the letter arrived in the post, with a conditional offer of BBC. The exam results came up trumps in August and we were in. University here we come. Now the excitement really begins.

3
After the exam results

The beginning of the greatest journey you will ever make

Unless you know me and are simply reading this book to see if you've got a mention, chances are you're actually preparing for university, and are a mix of excitement and nerves.

It's natural. You're stepping into the unknown, but trust me, do it right, read all the advice from here on in, and it will be absolutely brilliant.

A lot of the things you need to do before university are obvious, so I don't want to bog you down explaining what you should already know. However, I'll go through some of the basics, and some of the things you might not be aware of, and make sure you're well prepared.

> *TIP: Bursaries. Apply for everything. You never know, some company may give you some cash to do what you would be doing anyway.*

Funding

Make sure if you're from Scotland that you have applied to get your course fees paid for.

If you need a student loan, make sure you have applied well in advance for that too. You don't want to be moving to another city, and then waiting until October or even November to get your first loan payment. Apply before the end of July at the latest.

I got offered £800 for the year. That was going to be no good – I was now 23, had been working for three years prior to university, and would not be able to cash cheques from the bank of mum and dad every month.

That's another reason why you want to apply early. It meant I could appeal nice and quickly, which involved collecting all my wage slips, P60's etc, and posting them off. I eventually got my loan upped to a more reasonable £4300.

I also did my best to save up a bit of money before I went, and sold my car a few months after starting uni. If you can put a wee bit aside every week, even just have £500-£800 or so in your bank account when you leave, you'll be thankful for it if you find you're spending a little too much of your loan straight away.

You will learn to save money at uni. Split a bottle of vodka with four other people, have a few drinks to get you in the mood, and head out. Sometimes I went out with £10, bought drinks and food, had a great night and still came home with change.

> *TIP: Not so good at spelling? You best make sure you spell check and get people to proofread for you. There's nothing less professional or careless than a spelling mistake on final presentations.*

Part time job

Should you get one? Circumstances might state you have to. If you can, leave it for a few months, at least until the second semester.

You want to settle in and make friends with everyone in your halls. Being called away to work while everyone is out on the town or having parties sets you apart from everyone.

There is also the small point of having to adjust to university life. Although classes are not nine to five every day, it can still be a shock to the system with a glut of exams, assessments, presentations and essays to do, all for a variety of different subjects.

I'll touch on presentations in more detail in chapter 8, but what will become apparent is that if you're going to have to stand up in front of a classroom full of people and do a presentation, then you want to make sure that goes well.

You therefore want to be in a good group. Sometimes, that might even mean avoiding your mates if you know they aren't going to be reliable. There's nothing more frustrating about group work than having people who don't turn up to meetings. Even if your excuse is legitimate (ie you're working) you may struggle to get picked in that group again.

You can miss lectures and maybe even have a duvet day where you stay in bed and sleep off your hangover, but don't let down your group mates because you'll find it harder to pair up later on. Earn yourself a good reputation from the start by doing your fair share of work and doing a good presentation, then people will want to be in your group.

> *I graduated from Aberdeen in 2005 BEng Mechanical Engineering. I transferred from Robert Gordon's University's Mechanical and Offshore Engineering after second year. Aberdeen was better in every way, but RGU have bucked up their ideas since and are probably better from a facilities point of view, but you still can't beat the vibe and history of the old Aberdeen campus.*
>
> *Colin Struthers*

It is also worth considering that most places will want you to work over Christmas. Being from Aberdeen got me no favours with the festive rota.

For two years in a row, I found myself spending Christmas Day alone in an empty Glasgow flat because I couldn't get off work, while family were celebrating 180 miles up the road in Aberdeen.

It's actually pretty unthinkable it happening to you even once, but twice in a row there I was glumly sitting down to Christmas dinner by myself.

No exchanging gifts, no kids running round with their new toys, no-one to get drunk with.

All because I had bosses who demanded I work either Christmas Eve or Boxing Day, and it's a tad difficult to get public transport to the other end of the country around that time of year.

I'm not too bothered about Christmas, and/or family get togethers, so don't feel sorry for me. The only thing that depressed me was that the TV was rubbish and I had no friends to go drinking with because they were all students who had, funnily enough, gone home for Christmas.

I was just a bit annoyed more than anything because on both occasions my work didn't even need me, we were not even close to being busy, and they had plenty of Glasgow based staff who could have worked instead.

We're talking two different jobs here too – it wasn't even the same boss.

The first time I accepted it because the majority of the staff were working (even if we were well over staffed), but the second time there were only four of us, with another 16 Glasgow based staff given it off!

The manager closed early because we weren't busy, meaning we wouldn't even get the double time wages we were meant to be on.

He offered us all a free drink "to celebrate". I told him to shove it, put my coat on, and walked out.

What I should have known is that when you're under the age of 25, you can pretty much pick your job in a bar or restaurant. They're always employing, and they're always employing people your age.

If I'd put my foot down and refused to do it (and with good reason, even Ebeneezer Scrooge never made someone else spend Christmas by themselves) and they'd sacked me for it, I could have come back to Glasgow in January and walked into another job.

Like I said though, it wasn't that big a deal to me, I wasn't sat crying into my turkey.

I was more annoyed that I'd consoled myself with the extra wages and didn't even get them.

Working New Year is fine - in fact given how much New Year is built up and ultimately disappoints I actually preferred working it. Christmas though generally isn't worth it, at least in first year when you're already adjusting to living away from home, so make sure you're free to go home for the holidays.

I would suggest looking to get a job in January for the first time, and just try and save up enough cash before going to uni to tide you over for the first few months.

If you do have a job over Christmas, ask well in advance for it off, making sure you make them aware you live far from home. Offer to work New Year as a bargaining tool.

If they refuse, tell them your parents have told you to quit because you can't miss Christmas at home – knowing fine well even if they call your bluff you'll have little problem getting a job when you return.

References are important of course so you don't want to be leaving places on bad terms, but in reality this only becomes an issue when you're applying for jobs related to your career.

When it comes to part-time student jobs, don't get yourself too stressed about it.

We'll touch on part-time jobs in more detail later.

> *I worked throughout my four years in Pizza Hut. I couldn't not work. I've always understood the importance of earning my own money and not having to rely on anyone else. I've never understood the attitude of relying on "mummy and daddy" once you're quite capable of having a job. I met quite a few people like that at uni. At one point I decided to get myself a bar job in a night club, for the sake of it really. That lasted a good few months, great experience, had fun, but my word I spent a good bit of time sleeping in uni! Get a job, yes, but do not let it affect your education!*
>
> *Ashley Johnston*

Gap year

This seems like a good time to suggest to you a gap year. Why go straight from five or six years of secondary school to university anyway?

Obviously there's no need to take as long as I did to go, but I certainly don't regret not going when I had just left school. Considering how immature I was at that age a gap year doing voluntary work might have woken me up and I'm sure I'd have come back a better man.

First up, if you are 17, and you don't turn 18 for a good while into your freshers year, then if you can I'd suggest referring entry for a year. It's not a big deal really so don't worry if you are 17 and have already signed up to a course, I'm just gently advising you'd be better waiting until you're old enough to drink.

If you're underage then you should be allowed into at least most of the student unions. This doesn't include everywhere though. Glasgow Caledonian for example got rid of their union shortly after I left and now use the top floor of a nightclub, so you can't get in if you're only 17.

A lot of unions will let you in if you are underage, but mostly only if you are a student at that university (generally, a student card gets you into any student union in the country).

Even if you're allowed into the union, you're not allowed to drink. The licensing laws still apply. You'll be watched very closely by the bar staff and security. A lot of places will give you a stamp if you're old enough so the kids can't get served. Get caught breaking the rules once and you might find yourself barred, which considering it's your student union – the social hub of the university – is not a great thing to be barred from.

You may, on a busy night, get away with sitting in the corner while your mates bring drinks over for you, but generally you'll find yourself the sober one.

Worse than that though, it surely doesn't need explained that entry to the nightclubs is a no-go? You are asked for ID at the door most of the time, and in freshers week they are extra vigilant.

Being under 18 means you miss out on a huge part of university life. One of my flatmates did not turn 18 until February in her first year, she had little chance of getting in anywhere, and essentially stayed in right up until her birthday while we were all hitting the town.

Just don't do it kids. And if you do, get some **good** fake ID prepared before freshers week.

> *TIP: Always ask if a shop or restaurant does student discounts. They don't always advertise it, but a quick flash of the matriculation card could get you a range of benefits. The same goes for club entry.*

A gap year gives you the opportunity to do a few things. There are the obvious round the world trips that, if you're loaded, you can do.

Thinking of your career though, it wouldn't hurt to get some work experience.

It will make your CV look a little more impressive for when you graduate, and also give you a greater understanding of the industry and save you making the wrong choice career wise.

A job will also be worthwhile if it saves you up enough cash to be able to forget about a part-time job at university for the first few months you're there.

More than anything though, I've told you university isn't as hard as you think, but then I did journalism which is a very practical course.

I can imagine studying Physics or Medicine will take a little bit more out of you.

> ***TIP:*** *Join the student newspaper if you **don't** want to be a journalist. It's good for your CV, and you'll learn some extra skills. If you grow into a certain role and if you perhaps become a features or fashion editor, then it will give you some responsibility too which you can talk about in interviews.*
>
> *If you **do** want to be a journalist, then look further than a student newspaper, which sometimes isn't edited by journalism students. Look to start your own magazine, website or podcast. A Student rag is likely to be quite restricted in what you can do.*

What to bring

I'm going to presume you're staying in university halls. If not then I'll be very disappointed with you.

Find out in advance from your halls if you need bedding or any plates/cutlery. This may seem obvious, especially for the high price you're paying, but you'll be amazed at places where you drive three hours down the road to find you suddenly need to go shopping to buy what you took for granted would be there.

You also don't want to be coming down the road with a big duvet or a TV in the car if you don't need one, because it'll take up valuable room. So phone them a few days before and check.

I took a TV with me, and it was handy enough for having something to watch when eating my dinner, but you'll generally never watch it. If you are watching a lot of TV, by yourself, then you're not doing first year right.

However, we were entitled to free internet connection if you had brought a laptop, which was a godsend for the social media sites which were just taking off at the time. It was Myspace in first year, which I only discovered halfway through. Then Bebo in second year. And eventually we all found our way onto Facebook.

If you're lucky, the internet package may even include a few TV channels exclusive to your halls. Some have been known to give you American TV programmes that aren't due to hit our screens for another six months.

Some halls will have a common room, complete with couches and a TV for everyone to watch. Brilliant for socialising and meeting new people. If they don't, you'll usually find someone's flat becomes the unofficial home for everyone to go to when something is on the telly.

> ***TIP:*** *If you're getting your course fees paid, you can only get them once for each year. So you can get first year paid once, but if you change degrees and have to re-start in first year, expect to pay for it the second time.*

Laptop

As you may well have noted above, investing in a laptop or Macbook will do you a lot of good at university, or an iPad or equivalent these days. I appreciate though it's not the cheapest of things to buy, so don't worry if you can't get one.

You can generally get internet connection in your halls though, which helps with the essays when the library is shut. It is also handy to have around university if all the computers in your library are full as you can usually connect to the uni Wifi with ease.

More importantly, it helps when you wish to download music or films because you can use the university's high speed internet. Result.

It should be said, I started university in 2005. The smart phone was pretty unheard of then – I may be wrong but I don't think the first iPhone came out until 2007. Never mind the iPad. So getting internet access and checking e-mails are a lot easier now.

Who knows what will be invented by the time I stop being lazy and actually publish this.

> *I studied Computer Science and then returned to Uni in 2010 to do my MSc in the same subject. The degree was worth it as IT is one of the few industries that is always growing and very rarely suffers during problematic economic times.*
>
> *To pass my initial degree, I studied a bit but probably not enough. My MSc was a different story as I was older, wiser and had a bigger hunger for the work.*
>
> *Colin Robertson*

Other things to bring

Ensure you have your documents to hand, ie passports and birth certificates. You'll maybe need these when registering on your course, or registering with a doctor. I registered with a doctor (I think everyone did) but I don't know anyone who ever used it, but it's handy to be able to go to one if you need to. Actually tell a lie, someone in our block in halls contracted measles, and there was an urgent notice that went round telling anyone who hadn't had it as kids to go get immunised.

Sometimes the surgery will actually come round the halls and register the students on the spot, but generally you'll have to go do it yourself.

You will also at one point probably need passport style photographs, which are used for a variety of things. The photo for your Matriculation card which you get in freshers week (your student card basically) is usually taken by a photographer on the spot, but sometimes you can beat the queue with a passport photo.

You also might need it for clubs, gym membership, or possibly a library card.

TIP: If you're staying at home, try and find someone else who is doing the same and offer to car share. Will split the cost of petrol money, and it's always nice having someone from your course to chat to on the way to university to tell you about the assessment you forgot all about.

Also, if you're car sharing, universities are sometimes obliged to give you a car parking space because you're essentially doing your bit for the environment. If they don't, then why not find a staff member who usually takes the bus and offer them a lift, then you've definitely bagged a free parking space. Don't blow your sparse student dosh on pay-and-display.

If you can afford it, a mini-fridge for your room isn't a bad idea. It's always handy to have some beers in your room chilled, and you can't always guarantee your alcohol won't get nicked if it's in the kitchen when one of your flatmates decides to have an impromptu party.

School uniform – you will need this. Can guarantee in freshers week there will be at least one school disco, and if there isn't then there will be more throughout the year. Therefore, bring your white shirt, school tie, and expect it to get written on with fake (or real if you're lucky) phone numbers.

On that note, considering you want to budget while at uni, it's maybe worth planning ahead and bringing something to wear on Halloween too. Also, there's always a pub golf for someone's birthday, so kit yourself out with a dodgy hat, plastic golf club, dodgy long tartan socks and a golf glove.

Bring toilet roll. Lots of it. You won't have a cleaner providing toilet roll and fresh towels every day, it's not a hotel. With a lack of car, you'll find toilet roll takes up a lot of room in the few bags you can carry on the long walk from the supermarket. If anyone from home ever comes to visit and asks if you want them to bring you something – ask for them bumper packs of toilet roll.

- Double check your course

Make sure you have read up on your course properly, because once you start it can sometimes be tricky to change.

One girl told me the story of how she took one of the many business studies degrees, and only on her first day did she realise that third year was a year long placement working in a different city (and in some cases, country) which she didn't want to do. She then had to go about changing her course straight away because she hadn't properly read the prospectus.

- BUT.....Don't be too prepared

This sounds daft, but you can be too prepared. I listened to the horror stories about how hard you have to work at university, and how organised you have to be if you wish to survive. I turned up on day one with a range of folders, punching holes in every handout and making that annoying snapping noise every time I filed them away in the middle of class. I was also collecting things that were meant to be read once and binned. I had no room for half the stuff, but kept convincing myself I would be reading every word of everything while studying for exams.

Obviously, organise the important notes you pick up along the way, especially if they are related to an exam or an essay. However, there's no need to turn up like a walking advert for WH Smith.

Good tip: Bring loads of "punched pockets" (google it). Fill your bag with them, use them to collect your notes, and they're also handy for transporting that essay you're carrying around uni all day. You will actually go through loads of these.

Also, bring A5 sized shorthand notepads, and use them to write your notes from lectures. Will again save you room and are easier to keep stored away for when the time comes that you need to use your notes for revision.

You basically want to separate the important stuff you get told from all the garbage you get.

You'll work out your own system eventually, but maybe it wouldn't be a bad idea to think how you're going to organise yourself from the first week onwards.

We're all different, we all learn in different ways. Essentially, we fit into three categories - audio, visual or kinetic learning.

For an example, imagine you're buying a phone:-

Audio: You'll prefer the salesman telling you about the phone and its features.

Visual: You'll prefer seeing how the phone works and its features, ie the salesman showing you.

Kinetic: You'll prefer holding the phone and working out yourself how it work and its features.

Work out how you prefer to learn, and use it as a base on how you're going to study for exams.

TIP: Forget about the weekends. Sunday – Thursday are the best nights out, that's when you're drinking for next to nothing. The weekends are for when you've got money in your pocket, roughly translated as when you've a job!

Making friends before you get there

Facebook has engulfed the lives of everyone so much that it may be quite easy to attempt to find out who your future course mates are.

Even then, I don't think it's that possible, and certainly not for finding out who your flatmates are. You can start a Facebook group entitled "Marketing at Abertay" but don't hold your breath for a glut of followers.

You could also phone ahead, try and talk the receptionist into giving you the names of your flatmates, then Facebook stalk them, but you never get to know anyone properly until you meet them so just relax and let fate take its course.

I'll be honest. I tried to make friends before I got there. I succeeded in getting to know three people. It did nothing for me as far as my university experience went.

UCAS had sent all new students a magazine, detailing all the things that make other university guide books obsolete. You know, the "get a student account, apply for a student loan, etc."

These are all important things by the way. Open a student account, then when you register at university and have in your hands both a letter confirming you study there, and the much coveted matriculation card, you can head to the bank and sort out an overdraft.

Depending on your bank, it should be an extra £1,000 spending money. Yes you'll need to pay it back one day, so probably best to spend wisely.

I'm not going to give you advice like "don't blow it all at once" and "try and save some money" etc because that's not what you're reading this book to be told.

As for what student account to go for. Well, things change, deals and offers change every year. Have a look about and see what best suits you. See which freebies will actually do you some good.

Some offer a cheap railway card which gets you a third off train fares. If you're going to be using trains a lot, then it's very useful. If you're not, then go for something you can make more use out of.

Anyway, I digress. Little magazine arrived, and being polite I flicked through it, and noticed an advert for a website titled newstudent.org.

I don't think the website runs any more (I did type in the address but nothing loaded up). In fact, the year proceeding me starting at university seemed to be the only year it was popular, which is a shame as it was quite a useful tool.

It was actually very good for finding out things. You registered for the six universities you had applied for, and this gave you access to a forum dedicated to that university. You then could post a topic, lets call it "journalism", and ask if anyone else had applied.

On the Glasgow Caledonian forum, it began as a boisterous, busy message board. There were even a glut of journalism applicants, and we all made cyber friends and were chuffed that we'd all be going to uni together.

Then the interviews started.

One guy announced he had an interview. We all wished him luck and begged him to tell us what was asked. He went to his interview, and posted a goodbye note a week later saying he had been rejected.

Goodbye pal.

And so this went on. Every couple of weeks when the course interviewed another batch of interviewees, someone would get an interview, write back and tell us all the questions, and then post days later to say they had been rejected.

It was like an online version of platoon.

One such girl, Sam, and I had made good friends I thought. We had compared CVs and previous work experience, and were both fairly confident we at least deserved an interview. Finally, after months of waiting, she got an interview.

She went, did her interview, told me how hard it was, then told me she had been rejected.

She eventually went on to study journalism at Stirling, hated her halls and moved out after a week, despite my pleas and advice on how to go and make friends. That's another story though.

I ended up being the last forum member to be interviewed, and of course made it onto the course, but by that time there was no-one left to tell. So much for making friends with all my course mates before starting.

There were still a few others who had been accepted for other courses, and with a few days to go before uni we'd vowed to meet up at some point, and two in particular, a girl and a guy, I said I'd definitely see.

In the end, the girl was alright, I saw her briefly in the first week, and then as luck had it she became friends with some of my friends, but unsurprisingly nobody is the same in real life as they are online and I can't say we were ever big mates.

The guy? He thought he was a bit of a geezer. I thought he was a twat, and a weird one at that, and that probably put me off meeting up with people I've met online for the rest of my life.

So, quick round up. Newstudent.org was great for getting stories about the course, hearing about interviews etc, and was definitely worthwhile, and if it was around now I'd recommend it. But it isn't, probably because it's all about Facebook these days.

However, don't worry about going out of your way to try and meet folk before you get to university, because you probably won't and it did me no good anyway. You will meet folk on day one and take it from there.

Instead, I was going to university cold turkey, as billy no mates, in a city three hours drive from home, and around five years older than your average student.

And I wouldn't have had it any other way.

4
The first weekend

The moment you've been waiting all summer for. The day you live away from your parents for the first time. The day you move in with strangers, hoping you'll get on because you'll be sharing a flat with them for the best part of ten months.

This isn't going on holiday with the school where you come back after a week. This is real life. Where you have to do the cooking, cleaning and ironing, but where you can invite your mates round at 3am for a party and not have to worry about mum and dad marching downstairs and kicking your pals out.

You can invite that girl/boy over, or feeling randy coming back from town you can go knock their doors. There's not even a walk of shame in the morning, it's just across the courtyard.

I've pleaded with you in a past chapter and I hope it's got through to you – you have to move into the official university accommodation.

You might turn up on day one, see that it's a dump, and your rich dad might be telling you he'll get you the flat of your dreams. You will live to regret it if you don't move into halls in first year though.

The majority of my best stories came from two things – living in halls, and nights out with my work pals.

Yes I had good times with people from my course. I went on holiday to Manchester and Malia with uni mates, and I spent four months working in Ayia Napa which brought its own set of stories.

I had some epic nights out working in two nightclubs in the city centre. There are stories I don't even remember because I was so drunk.

Nothing compares though to the considerable halls parties; the girls; getting drunk with your mates; the water fights; bringing home 14 traffic cones and blocking a friend in his room; trying to cook pasta with your equally drunk pal; getting the keys to the drunk birthday boys room and racing to get home before him so you can swap everything from his room with everything in the kitchen and forcing the poor guy to sleep there.

Going on a night out and on your way down the stairs knocking everyone's door and dragging them all out on the town with you. Knocking everyone's door on the way home and not having to worry about their angry parents answering.

I hated the mess. I hated it when dishes piled up, when people refused to empty the bin, or when you opened the fridge to an awful smell because someone had chicken a week out of date.

The humour of the fire alarm going off in the middle of the night died quickly, as did being woken up by flatmates coming home on them rare occasions you were in bed before them, or by your flat buzzer constantly going off because everyone has friends visiting at all times of the day or night. Sometimes it felt like I had no privacy, but then I liked being around people and you never felt alone.

Halls can be annoying at times. Your kitchen can descend into a war zone. Law of averages state you'll have at least one flatmate you detest. You might take a disliking to all of them.

You can have the best flat in the city though, but no-where near as many friends. You can throw a party and follow everyone around hoping your flat doesn't get wrecked, or throw one in halls and laugh when someone drops the bottle of wine.

University is just far better when you're in halls. You're only going to do it once. No-one regrets it.

Join a sports club. You may be forced to spend time in halls and classes with certain people, but it is in the clubs that you will find better mixes and people with similar views. Best bet is something like swimming. Good exercise, good competitive level against the other unis, cant be affected by weather and have you ever seen a good level swimmer without a cracking body?

Sports teams night outs are always legendary and the balls are even better. Don't limit yourself to just one club, but don't spread yourself too thin.

Colin Struthers

First up, most halls don't want 1,000 students firing down on the Saturday morning.

If they tell you to move in from Thursday, they know people will trickle down over the course of a few days.

Other halls might actually give different students a set moving in day or time. I actually think I was given a time of 2pm on that Thursday now that I recall. I turned up at 4pm. You can generally ignore these arrival times and arrive when you want into the chaos that ensures on that first week. If you can, try and be there on the first day.

I still had to work out how to get all my stuff to Glasgow from Aberdeen. As bad luck had it, my parents had booked a holiday around the time I was leaving for uni, so they were not around. My brother in law said he'd take me, but work meant he couldn't do it until the Saturday, and I was determined to be there on the first day.

A mate offered. He even offered to take me in his work van so I could bring more stuff. Then, it dawned on him what he was getting himself in for and he duly made his excuses. I didn't blame him, it's a 300 mile round trip with the only reward being some petrol money and a "Cheers mate, appreciate that."

Only one thing for it, I was going to have to drive myself down and move in by myself.

One thing I wish I'd thought to do was book a parking space at the halls. I didn't, and got shafted out onto the side streets, in pay and display, where I had to carry everything – including the TV which I didn't need – from what felt like half a mile away and then up the stairs to the top floor. That wasn't fun.

Again, this will vary from university to university. You might have halls where the security guards, receptionists, staff etc are only too happy to have you. Others have taken the job for the money and generally can't be bothered with another year of teenagers causing them hassle.

Don't be over anxious about it though. You're stressed out already, you're being told that you'll have to park on pay and display for the next two weeks, at about £12 per day, until your parents can come down for the first time and pick up the car, and you're maybe feeling a little unwelcome. Just try and take it on the chin and work out a solution – there is always a solution. If anything, it's given you a conversation topic to break the ice with when you meet your new flatmates.

As it goes, I did manage to trick the security guard and sneak the car in when he left the gate open for a few brief moments.

Here I give you some more advice. If you have a car, don't take it with you. You see, you will become the designated taxi driver. The one who has to take everyone to the supermarket. The one who gets a phone call at 3am asking for a lift. The one who is asked to drive to the gig because it's raining. The one who is convinced to take the car to that flat party across town, and to "just leave the car there and pick it up in the morning" only to find you've a bright yellow parking ticket on it the next day.

The one who has to then explain to the security guard that your car has been in the car park all along because you booked a parking space and to let you back in.

Don't do it. Even the two weeks I had the car were a nightmare. The car is handy in second and third year when you only live with three or four friends as opposed to 200 in first year, and you might have a free parking space too, but until then it's just a hindrance.

Never mind that though, it's our first day in halls.....

> *I was the second one in our flat to arrive on move in day. The first was a guy I ended up living with the majority of my student life and we were pretty much inseparable until I moved to London after uni. Despite the old cliche that you make lifetime friends with those you live with at uni, I found that we were in the minority as I cant think off the top of my head many others who became best mates with their original flat mates.*
>
> *Once I was unpacked we waited in the kitchen talking about who we might be living with. We both had requested a mixed flat so were getting optimistic about being two lads in with six girls. The next to arrive was a quiet 'unusual' guy who went straight to his room. Then a 6ft 4 yank guy straight out of an American teen movie. Our odds diminished every time the door opened. It got to a stage where there were five guys in the kitchen (one still in his room) when the realisation came that there were going to be no girls in our flat.*
>
> *We basically embraced this blessing in disguise and had a great year just doing what guys do; a year long party.*
>
> *Craig Forson*

As I was driving down the road, I was imagining what my flatmates would be like. My flatmates turned out to be nothing like I imagined they would.

My main worry was that being a mature student, I'd get a mature student flat, and would actually be in a flat with over 40's, and/or with people who had no interest in embracing the student lifestyle.

Thankfully, my worries were unfounded. Instead I got a 17 year old, three 18 year olds, and a 22 year old. I was the oldest (and Grandad was a name I got used to being called) but was comfortably within the same age bracket.

Don't take it for granted though – if you're in the same boat (ie mature student – you young 'uns can just leave it to fate) then phone ahead two weeks before starting, and ask who they've put you in a flat with. You might be in my boat and worried about being in a mature flat. You might be the other way around and actually want to avoid teenagers. Don't leave it up to the day you arrive, because changing flats can sometimes be a lengthy experience, and if halls are full then you'll find it difficult to get moved at all, and even if you do it might not be to an improved room/flat.

Firstly, on moving in day, you get there and realise the place is never organised enough for you. I stood in a long queue, got handed keys in an envelope that simply said "Nairn 325". That was as good as it got – others arrived and didn't have a room designated to them yet and the office staff were deciding where to put them.

At least I had my keys though. I walked out of reception, looked round campus, and had little idea where I was going.

I worked out Nairn stood for the block I was in, so 325 must therefore be my room number. Easy eh? Except I walked in to find there were two doors to each floor, and only three floors. Maybe you're reading this and you've worked out straight away that the number 325 clearly meant third floor, flat two, room five. I didn't. I simply guessed it must be the third floor, then tried my key in both doors until one unlocked, then was actually surprised I had walked into a flat as I expected to have to do a bit more searching.

That was my first experience. Secondly, you may get given a form when you apply for halls asking you basic details like name, age, course, and whether you want en-suite or non-en suite. They may even ask you to include a photo. That bit is fine. The next part of the form is useless, and this seems to be a common occurrence for most universities and wasn't unique to mine.

You may be asked to describe your hobbies, even what sort of flatmate you'd like to be put with - whether you want a mixed flat or ones that are all the same sex. This gives you the impression you're choosing to be with like minded people.

You may as well write down that your favourite hobby is fornicating with different types of cheese, you'd like to live with an Austrian goat herder, and would be more comfortable living with five people who haven't decided what sex they are yet. No-one pays any attention to your choices. Remember a few paragraphs ago, where they were still handing out random keys on the day? Others had ticked the boxes for mixed flats and got given a single sex one.

Best advice, don't try and be funny on your form (ie ignore my last paragraph), and just put some sensible stuff down, and let them put it on the pile with the rest of them. Don't make your form stand out as if you get someone reading it who has no sense of humour - who knows where they'll put you.

> ***TIP:*** *If you get homesick, the best thing to do is go do something. Homesickness always hits you the worst when you're by yourself, or staring at four walls in your depressing looking bedroom.*
>
> *Go do something you couldn't do before. That might be a walk into town, a drink with friends, a trip to the cinema, or just explore your new town/city. Remind yourself of the good things leaving home brings and enjoy your new freedom and surroundings.*

So I was in my flat. I had visions of walking into a living room of fresh faced boys and girls, all sat on a sofa, with a bottle of vodka already opened, and my arrival prompting cheers and hugs from my sexy new pals.

If that happens to you, then fair play to you, you've won the lottery. In reality, most of you will have to lower your expectations a little.

It's rarely like entering the Big Brother house and walking down the stairs to excited housemates. Instead, I opened the door to a dark, empty corridor, staring at six bedroom doors, and one to my immediate left marked kitchen.

Kitchen it was then, this will be where everyone is. Now it looked decent enough, two of most things (two ovens, two sets of hobs, two sinks). It also had a large fridge/freezer surprisingly big enough for six people, plenty of cupboards and cooking space, a large dining table and a lovely view of the motorway.

Okay so the view wasn't great, but that's just picking hairs. In general, it was alright, and I quickly went to work finding an empty cupboard to make my own.

No flatmates, though I could hear the faint sound of music, so knew someone had moved in.

I found my room, which wasn't as grand as the kitchen – a small, thin room with a single bed in the corner; but I had a desk; an office chair; a comfier cushion chair; a wardrobe; a board for pinning photos, posters and timetables to, and best of all an en-suite bathroom which became a novelty I would grow to love and adore.

Yes, it was small and I knew once everything was unpacked there wouldn't be much room to maneuver, but there were no horrifying stains, leaks or smells. I was actually pretty impressed, this was going to be alright.

I'd been told to leave my door open so it was easier to meet your flatmates, as clearly a closed door gives an unfriendly impression. My flatmates hadn't got that same memo but I put a door stopper underneath and kept it open, and went to work on the long (and it was long) job of retrieving stuff from my car and hauling it to my room.

I thought, with people having already moved in, they would have already introduced themselves to each other and were now simply unpacking. I found out later no-one had yet met anyone. In fact as I was walking out of the flat, a young girl walked past me, said hello, then hurried to her room. I didn't even get her name and this was a girl I was going to be living with for the best part of a year.

Anyway, let's get moved in, unpacked, and then I can get to know them all when they resurface.

Back and forth I went trying to get all my stuff, and on the way kept bumping into people in the corridors. I'd introduce myself, help the girls up the stairs with some boxes, then be given the heartbreaking news they weren't my flatmates.

At least I'd met the neighbours though, and as it turned out they became better friends than the people I was living with, so try make a good impression with absolutely everyone – smile, offer to help, and make some small talk.

In truth, although you obviously want to be friends with your flatmates, it's not that big a deal. We had eight flats in our little block "Nairn", with six students to a flat. That was 47 potential friends right there, plus all the other blocks, not to mention the people you'll meet on your course, workmates when you eventually decide to get a part-time job, friends you meet at parties, friends of friends, and so on.

Really, I spent a summer worried what my flatmates would be like for no reason. As long as they aren't a nightmare to live with then you'll be fine.

> *I lived in Cairncross Halls in Glasgow. It is a classic 'halls' in that none of the accommodation was self-contained flats but rather floors of bedroom doors and several shared kitchens. Most residents had to share a room. Sharing a room with a stranger could have had its difficulties but I was sharing with a friend from school (arranged beforehand) so I already had a friend.*
>
> *The first night we were sitting in our room when a couple of girls knocked on our door and said that people were meeting in the common room (one common room for the entire accommodation block) and then going out. We went down and joined them. There were loads of people which naturally broke up into smaller groups and we all had a few drinks. Then we went out to a club.*
>
> *Joanne (my roommate) and I met a few people that night but got chatting to one guy called James who we arranged to meet the next day. We never got rid of him after that and we lived with him for two more years.*
>
> *Laurann De Verteuil*

Once I'd everything up from the car, my friend Laurann came round to "help". Her timing as ever was impeccable, managing to arrive just as I'd finished. The two of us though decided we'd go and meet the flatmates.

Flatmate number one was the same girl who had ran past me in a hurry earlier. She was 17, and a nursing student. Within the space of a few minutes she would tell us - numerous times - that she had a boyfriend, as if she was warning me off her. In fact she talked about him that much I thought they'd been going out for years and were on the verge of marriage – they had been together for two weeks, and I think broke up within days.

In the space of a few hours on that first night, she would tell us she had been having an affair with her teacher, attempt to sleep with what later became my mate Craig, storm into the kitchen/living room and announce to us all after the attempted seduction didn't work "I threw myself at him and he wasn't interested", and generally do everything a young girl probably shouldn't do on her first night in halls.

After the two week romance fizzled out, a good friend from the flat downstairs quickly became besotted with her. Granted now she was a good looking girl, but he went off her the night she got drunk in one of our flat parties, and proceeded to spend the evening lying in bed being sick all over herself, and him.

Bless her little heart though, she was a car crash waiting to happen at times, but generally she was harmless. In my opinion she went to university a year or two early and should have waited until she was a little more mature.

The next flatmate was an 18 year old lad from Edinburgh. He seemed friendly enough to be fair and any time he was around we got on well, but we barely saw him all year. He had rich parents back home and spent much of his time in what I presume was a penthouse apartment complete with swimming pool and back garden amusement park, having his butler drive him to Glasgow every day.

Even on that first night, he stayed for a few hours, then ran off to the west end of the city to meet his pals at another university to make friends with their flatmates. That was a bad mistake. People used to ask me who my flatmates were, and when I said his name hardly anyone knew who he was. I'm sure he had a great time with his pals at another halls, but he missed an opportunity to make more friends right on his doorstep.

Next up was a second girl. She was a character. Entertaining, but one of those girls you'd maybe rather was your neighbour than living with you. She (well, all the flatmates really) was also an absolute nightmare when it came to keeping the place clean. The dishes piled up that bad once that one flatmate set his pan on fire, couldn't find any space in either sink, and so had no choice but to throw it on the floor, burning a nice black circle on it.

She was though a bit more confident than the rest, and that came in handy on that first night when it was a case of knocking doors and going to parties.

Flatmate number four was another girl. She had arrived earlier, dropped off her stuff, and would be returning Sunday. She should never have went near halls. She hated the noise, hated the social scene; she basically hated students. We barely saw her. She would hide in her room, even when we knocked on her door inviting her out she would open it only enough to poke her face through it, make her excuses, and close it quickly.

Even in the kitchen we only saw her twice a week. She would cook a vegetable stir fry, making enough to last for three days, put it in a plastic tub, and bring it to her room which presumably she kept in a mini-fridge. While cooking she would also tut loudly at you for cooking meat, judging you for having a cheeseburger.

She eventually moved out in January, moving into a different block to live with more like minded young ladies. I barely saw or spoke to her again.

Funny thing is, I probably made more effort to get on with her than any of the other three already mentioned. She wasn't having it though. She was that much of a recluse, good friends of mine who lived in the same block, and were even regularly in my flat, still think I made her up because they never saw her.

That was all the flatmates except one. Room number six was empty. We knocked, no-one answered. It would remain a short mystery to be answered later on.

Mum and Dad left me off. We all realised that all the sockets where low wattage and none of my appliances fitted them. Dad had to go to B&Q to sort it all out!

We were given an apartment inside the halls, eight rooms to one kitchen. My wee apartment, in which we were all nursing students, became my friends for my time at uni and are still good friends now.

The halls were pretty basic but comfortable and a great way to meet people who are all in the same boat.

I was quite homesick during the first week, but during my first weekend home, I couldn't wait to get back to halls as I'd been having so much craic.

Cathy Robinson

Like I said, it doesn't matter who your flatmates are, because the whole of your accommodation is there waiting to be made friends with. Your flatmates are merely the first people you introduce yourself to, and someone to go knocking on doors with. I ended up becoming best friends with one of the flats two floors below us, so much so that I ended up living with three of the six people in that flat the next year.

At times I even cooked most of my dinners down there; was a cleaner kitchen and they had a TV in the living room, and they had moved all the comfy chairs that were meant to be in the bedrooms into the kitchen to create a cosy seating area for everyone to relax and chat away. It became the social hub for everyone – and we all just headed down there every day, no matter what time it was, to chill out, catch up, and make plans for the next night out.

Now, if you've no problem socialising, then you know how to make friends. However many will read this and perhaps have had an awkward time at school, and will be hoping that university is the chance to reinvent yourself. I'm pleased to inform you, that's true. You can be whoever you want to be in a different town.

I'm not going to tell you every friendship I made that night. It was a haze of drink, of moving about to different parties, and of meeting the mystery sixth flatmate from our flat in a drunken stupor.

It was a good night. I had a few beers but didn't get drunk too early. I knew it would be a night of making a good first impression so I paced myself, kept the drinking sociable, and only late on when everyone else was making the effort to get drunk did I join them.

Remember, you're meeting people for the first time, and you're trying to make friends. You met people on that night covered in sweat, swaying from side to side, and dribbling absolute nonsense. Chances are, you're not going to stand around and make friends with them unless you really want a mate that goes around covered in sweat any time he has a few drinks and sees an attractive member of the opposite sex. You'll have plenty of time in freshers' week to hit bottle after bottle, and you'll have some legendary drunken nights all through uni. Don't try and impress anyone with your drinking skills that first night, just drink enough to kick you out of your shyness and go say hello to people.

Besides, it's the first night of what is going to be an incredible four years. Try and remember it. It's something to look back on and remember the first time you met all your future best mates. Who knows, you might even meet your husband/wife on that first night.

> *My first night was actually pretty easy, I arrived around 5pm on the Saturday to be greeted by three of my flat-mates all laughing and joking with each other. They all came and greeted me at the door and gave me a hand with bringing my possessions in from the car which was really helpful, it all happened in a blur really... I was really nervous about moving away but within the first hour of arriving in my flat, I knew I had made the right decision. That very first night we held a flat party where there must have been 20/30 people there. I met people that night which are still close to me this day.*
>
> Danny Collins

So, back to you, the shy 17 year old who is starting university and is terrified of leaving the only friends you ever had back at home.

Firstly, your best friend at home could have been your teddy bear, or you could have been the most popular person in your town. Everyone is starting university in the same boat – save for the very few people who have actually moved into halls with someone they know. Generally we're all on our own on that first night. And no-one knows anything about you, so you've just started a new life with a clean slate.

Here's my top tips to ensure you become Mr (and Miss) popular in the first few weeks.

Firstly, you will open every conversation with the same lines. You will ask the same four questions, and your new pal will ask you the same four. It's boring, its repetitive, but it's how everyone breaks the ice.

So, be prepared for hundreds of "What's your name", "What flat you in", "What course are you studying on", "Where you from" and if you're lucky even a "How old are you?"

Here's the thing. Of all the people you speak to on that first night, you'll only ever remember a few. You just meet far too many people. You'll make friends with someone, then go to another party (there'll be more than one, and you'll be welcome at all of them. You might even be hosting one of the parties) and you'll get into a deep conversation with someone else that you think you're going to be good friends with, only to never see or speak to them again.

Unless you're on the same course as that person or in the same block of flats, very few people will remember your name or anything else you've told them. It's not ignorance, I woke up the next day to texts from people I couldn't picture, and walked down the street past a range of hellos from people I didn't even remember meeting.

However, the reason I was getting these texts and hellos was down to a rather simple little trick.

Once you've got speaking to someone for five minutes, and have come to the conclusion they seem a decent sort and aren't likely to be asking to try on your mum's clothes to satisfy a weird fetish, get their number.

Don't make a big deal out of it. Don't say "Can I have your phone number because I really like you and I think we could be really good friends." That's weird. Don't do that.

Just say a simple "You'll need to give me your number, I'll give you a shout when our flat is having a party."

Trust me, the more numbers you can get the better.

You can of course add them on Facebook, but then that draws you in to becoming an online friend. Let's be honest, we've all got people on our Facebook friends list we wouldn't even say hello to if we walked past them in the street.

Get the phone number, it'll encourage you to actually meet up with these people within the next day. Don't leave it a week, they won't remember you. Ask them out for a pint that weekend, tell them to bring their flatmates up to your gaff for an impromptu party, tell them you're going clubbing that night and do they and their flatmates fancy coming. Makes friends with them basically. The more pals you've got the better life generally is.

Another trick which I worked out by accident, but what worked like a treat, is to introduce yourself using your nickname. I did it because the first guy I met outside our flat was called Andy, a Northern Irishman who as it happened came from the same small town half my family do, which got us talking.

Only one of Andy's flatmates had turned up on the Thursday, and she was one of those who shouldn't have bothered moving into halls. To move in on your first day, refuse to go out on that first night and instead stay confined to your room, and in the next ten months make little effort to meet anyone new – it's the wrong thing to do. The only person she seemed to interact with was her strange boyfriend who we dubbed the asylum seeker because he pretty much moved in without paying any rent, but we never got to know him because he was always hidden in her room. The flatmates would actually come home to find he was in the flat and she wasn't – he was just sat in her room all day waiting for her like a puppy dog.

Amazingly, she wasn't the only one. There were so many people in halls who were content to sit in their rooms all year and forget all about the social scene.

We're all different, and what is good for one person is annoying for another, but it can't be a pleasant experience alienating yourself from day one. Make an effort, it doesn't hurt.

If your problem isn't ignorance, and it's simple shyness or lack of confidence, then get reading a book on overcoming it. What you'll find though, is that it's easy to make friends in the first week because no-one's judging you, they're just out to make as many friends as possible, and you can hang around with a big group of people without saying very much and it'll be fine.

You don't have to be the life and soul of the party, just be at the party!

Be sociable and be seen. Don't hide away, and your confidence will grow the more you hang around with the same people, as will your number of friends.

Back to Andy, whose new flatmate wasn't for being convinced to go anywhere, and the other four rooms stayed empty – three moved in later that weekend and the fourth after a big fight broke out in her original flat.

Sat alone in his room with a six pack of beer, he took the decision to go knocking doors by himself, went to the party across the hall where I happened to be, and I was the first person he spoke to. He's never left me alone since.

We couldn't both go party hopping with the same name though, so I said "Just call me Panda" - which was my nickname from back home.

It actually helped. No-one remembers the thirty Daves they met that night, or the glut of Sarahs, or all the Lauras.

However, not many people forgot the name Panda. And also apart from the mundane questions about where I was from, what course I was doing etc, I had something else to talk about.

And so everyone remembered my name, and everyone had my phone number. For the first few weeks I had a good number of people texting me to ask if anyone was having a party, if anyone was heading to that freshers night at the union, if anyone wanted to go register at the doctor, go searching for the nearest supermarket, etc.

That's all you need. A mobile phone, some alcohol, and a mouth to say hello with. A nickname is a bonus, but you'll find you'll get lumped with a nickname soon enough, even if they aren't always the most original. There was Geordie Joe and Geordie Steve, Irish Craig, Dunblane Sarah, Belfast Beth, Ginger Martin, Optom Dave, Twin Claire, Craig Killie, Steve Nutter – oh no wait that wasn't a nickname, that was his actual name.

No-one, unless they have a name like Ifeoma that isn't very common, will ever be known simply as Laura or Mike. It's just how it is.

My first night in halls was amazing, in fact the first week as a whole is one of my best memories from uni.

My mum dropped me off, and she sat my bags in my room and left. There was no hanging round or emotional goodbyes.

I felt a sudden sense of responsibility, which made me apprehensive for all of five seconds before it quickly turned to excitement. I hated my room to begin with, and actually felt a little depressed about being left to live there, but by the time I had my stuff in it and posters up I loved it.

Looking back the living room was appalling; I don't know how I sat on those sofas and watched that TV for a full year, and we also had to put up with beetles coming out the lift shaft, but at that time none of it mattered.

I already knew all my flatmates and the first thing we did was go to Tesco. Three of us had forgotten to pack a duvet, and we needed to stock up on Tesco value freezer meals and cider, because of course we thought as students we were skint. We weren't.

After that two boys (the author of this book was one of them) invited us to a party and that started off at least two years of going out five nights a week!

Natalie McDougall

Foreign students

I found it quite alarming how anti-foreign we all were. People were actually fearful of having a foreign flatmate, like it was some sort of disease.

The foreign students that do descend on university are generally split up, in order to help integrate them into Scottish society. That meant in the flats of six that we had, usually one was foreign.

All I can say is I would never wish to be a student coming to live in Scotland, because we may see ourselves a friendly country, but in reality we're not as welcoming as we'd like to think we are.

No-one seemed to like their foreign flatmates; whether they were French, Spanish, German or Indian.

In our flat, it turned out mystery flatmate number six was Jorge, a manic haired Spaniard who looked identical to Barcelona's Carlos Puyol.

I met him first by accident at the end of the first night parties. The drink that had been passed around had taken their toll and I was stumbling all over the place, and stumbled into a group of Spaniards.

They were sadly all huddled together outside, because they weren't being made that welcome at any of the parties.

So much for friendly and welcoming Scotland.

Anyway, in my drunken haze I told them I'd look out for them all, and that if anyone hassled them to come and see the Panda.

I told them my flat number, may have kissed one of them on the cheek, and slapped another's arse, and stumbled off rather proud of myself that I'd improved Scottish-Spanish relations and unashamed at the slightly homoerotic welcome.

Two minutes later I was back in my kitchen, with a party going on around me, watching my flatmate sat in her underwear on Andy's lap, telling us all about her failed coup at trying to make Craig the first notch on her bedpost. Then a group of loud Spaniards walked in behind me.

Now, I tried explaining that I was only joking outside and that chances are I wouldn't be able to sort anyone out that was bullying them.

However, young Jorge was amongst them, mystery flatmate number six.

The Spanish sat down, and to a man and underwear clad woman, everyone else made their excuses and left, put off by the thought of having to speak to foreigners.

The thought of it, people speaking in a different accent to them. The horror.

Now I'll be honest, I was just out to try and make friends that night, and didn't want to be left out as everyone headed off to another flat.

But, I looked at my new Spanish friends, saw the sad look in their eyes and that same sigh they had probably done many times that night, and thought I'd make the effort.

After all, what are we all so worried about? They're foreign, they still love the same things we do.

"So...............Real Madrid or Barcelona?"

That kicked off the conversation, and it went on from there.

You see, Jorge had more brains in him than the rest of our sorry flat put together. He was a massive football fan, which suited me down to the ground. Him and his mates also turned out to be cracking pals.

If you've never eaten Spanish food, I urge you to. Having your own Spanish pals cook for you is a godsend. Cheese on toast was replaced by Spanish omelettes and a obsession with Chorizo.

Also, because Jorge was in a different country, and his fears were ten times what mine had been, he appreciated having a Scottish amigo more than anyone in halls. And if you look after your fellow man, he will look after you.

In a six person flat, who knew the one I'd speak to the most would be the crazy Spaniard, and he was crazy.

He had wild hair, dipped his toast into his coffee, had a mad Iberian temperament that usually came to the fore when you woke him up during his 5pm siesta, but that just made him even more likeable.

So, promise me this. If you have a foreign flatmate or one living nearby, and you think he or she is a bit weird, their English is rubbish, and their ways and attitude to life is a little different to what you're used to - don't ignore them, embrace them.

Put yourselves in their shoes and imagine you were the foreigner in their country. It would be nice if at least one person made the effort with you.

Trust me. That awkward foreign may well turn into the best friend you ever make at university.

> *Glasgow, it was one of the best years in my life.*
>
> *At the beginning I was a little bit nervous because I had never studied for a whole year in a different country.*
>
> *Before I arrived in Glasgow, I wrote to the Caledonian University just to know the most important things about Glasgow life. They sent me a report about the current students in the university, they told you where u can live, the main streets, supermarkets, public transports, and so on.*
>
> *I went to Glasgow with three more students from Zaragoza, so it was easier for me. We decided to stay in the Caledonian residence, just five minutes walk from the university. I think it was the best option, because it was there where I met a lot of people from different countries.*
>
> *Every Wednesday we went to a Erasmus meeting, where you could meet a lot of people; maybe it was the principal way to meet people.*
>
> *The principal problem was the language. Scottish people has a very difficult accent...they speak very quickly (Spanish people too) and I remember the first day I arrived that I was thinking of coming back to Spain because I couldn't talk with anybody. It was horrible.*
>
> *But....I only have very good words about my year in Glasgow. I met a lot of people, I learned how to life alone, I improved my English...everything was great!*
>
> *I love Glasgow and Scotland!*
>
> *Jorge Martinelli, Carlos Puyol lookalike*

Stay safe

Not everyone going to all these parties are particularly good people. Also, not everyone going to the parties are even students.

No-one knows anyone. Therefore, any random can go to a party, say they're a student, get in your front door, maybe even your bedroom, and you'll think nothing of it.

Firstly, always lock your bedroom door.

The way our flats worked, if people were at a party and wanted to go to the toilet they had to use an en-suite in someone's room. Best thing to do is keep your door locked, and if someone you know (or at least someone you've got to know fairly well) asks to use the toilet then go with them (ie open the door, and sit on the bed while they go).

Don't trust anyone with your room keys yet.

Best thing to do really is keep it to a select few people you trust. Who wants to spend a party chaperoning people to and from the toilet?

Further than that, if you are a girl, don't be by yourself with guys you don't know.

I remember being at a party, and my two male flatmates and I nipped back to the flat since we lived just upstairs to get more beer.

As we walked in one of the girls we lived with was stood in our flat hallway just outside her room talking to three guys.

One was pushing his way into her room, while she gave me that look that said "Get them out of here". One of his two mates, stood outside the room like a guard dog, said "It's alright mate, they're fine."

Looking back I was probably lucky I didn't get my head kicked in as I went steaming into the room, barging the guard dogs out of the way, and told the guy to get out. Thankfully they left without too much bother.

He was a bit angry about it, but I think his two guard dogs had eyed up my flatmates - one a rugby player and the other a six foot plus goalkeeper with mad Spanish hair, and didn't fancy it.

It turned out the three guys weren't even from our halls and were actually second year students staying elsewhere, but they knew there would be parties in our accommodation in that first week and knew young drunk freshers are easy prey.

So be careful who you let into your flat. Try to stay in a group of people who you know are definitely living there.

It's hard because you don't know anyone and it's difficult to know who to trust, but it's another reason not to get too drunk on the first night.

That doesn't mean you have to start with a big distrust of everyone of the opposite sex. Happily, 99% of people you meet will be just fine.

I would say my biggest regret initially was having a boyfriend that I constantly went home to visit. I wish I had spent more weekends in Glasgow as a student. Your student days are for enjoying being young, carefree and single. That said I had a fantastic time and some very memorable nights.

One being the food/toothpaste fight that broke out between Sarah and I (the only two girls, unless you count the other one we don't mention!) against the three boys resulting in my mattress being thrown down the stairs, and a very angry French man from next doors flat shouting at the boys "That's not how you treat a lady!"

The usual capers of a student stealing absolutely anything you can get your hands on a night out, I think the best was 14 traffic cones in one night.......funny at the time, perhaps not the next day when you have security banging at your door.

Emma Rochford

What it if all goes wrong?

Lets remember Sam, the Stirling student who didn't quite enjoy halls as much as I did and left early.

It's very easy to be told "Go and make friends." It's like telling people "Go and chat up that girl at the bar," something most people can't actually do. It sounds easy on paper, but plucking up the courage is a lot harder in practice.

I genuinely think you'd need to be desperately unlucky not to make friends in halls. Sam's problem though was her halls were not flats, they were just bedrooms in a corridor. If you've maybe moved in late it is harder to make friends and you're a bit excluded. That wasn't a problem in our halls because the late arrivals had flatmates who would then introduce them to friends they'd made.

All you need to do though is make one friend. You won't make any friends by sitting in your room. If halls have not come up trumps, or you don't even live in uni accommodation, then freshers week is your friend.

You will get offered the chance to join so many clubs. Be it sports clubs, or shared interests club, or societies. Make sure you join one. I actually joined the skiing club, then never bothered going, but I'm strange like that.

I joined badminton because I remembered being not bad at it when I was at school. I went twice, realised my memory was playing tricks on me and I was in fact rubbish at it, and I never went back.

I did though create a team and joined the five-a-side football league. We were rubbish, which was never more evident than when the fixture list threw up a clash with Jorge and his Spanish pals and we got thumped about 30-0, but it was a laugh and kept me fit.

If you are rubbish at a sport, don't let that put you off. Anyone from my year at Glasgow Caledonian could not fail to remember good old Canadian John. Canadian John was no David Beckham. In fact, he was no Victoria Beckham when it came to football skills.

He turned up at football trials, was told politely he wasn't good enough to make the team, but turned up every week at training and matches anyway. He never had any hope of getting a game, and on the training pitch was an embarrassment, but he was determined to get involved.

It worked out well for him. At the end of the year all the sports teams got invited on a week long trip to Spain. Canadian John joined the party, and in a sex fueled week of debauchery, our little friend struck lucky – not just anywhere, but in the middle of the dance floor. I don't mean lucky as in he got a cheeky kiss – I mean lucky as in she was happy enough to cut her knees open on the broken glass on the floor while she, well, you know. There's a photo of it - I really wanted to put it in this book but its not for public viewing, your parents wouldn't approve.

> *There's always a few people who are magnets to other people and their room, by extension, becomes like a drop-in centre. These are the people you need to get involved with.*
>
> *Steve Kerr*

I joined the gym, and university gym membership is worth it because it's cheap. It also houses gorgeous looking women in skimpy outfits. And, if you are already are a woman (or just like men), then fit men, and plenty of men who think they're fit.

While we're on that, if you are gay, be open about it, because you'll actually find there's a very open gay community at university. I met some very weird and wonderfully eccentric gay men and woman. It's not like school where it'd be almost social suicide to reveal you were homosexual. University life is more grown up, so don't worry about it.

> *My first day in halls I was known as the secret housemate as although I had moved my belongings to halls on the first day we could (Thursday), I didn't actually stay there until the Sunday night. At which point all of my flat (well most of them) had already bonded and got to know all of our neighbours.*
>
> *I think when I arrived with a bottle of vodka and asked where the party was that night, then I fitted in instantly.*
>
> *Moving into halls was my first time living away from my parents and it normally is everyone else's as well. They are normally absolute dives, worse than a cheap holiday inn, but everyone is in it together.*
>
> *So the first few weeks were a bit mental (picture a hotel in Malia, Corfu, Magaluf etc) as everyone basically gets drunk and parties with their new mates. This combined with freshers week is the easiest time to pull or at least lay the ground work for later in the year.*
>
> *Rule 101 of halls (and it's so easily done) – don't sleep with your flatmate/neighbour on the first night, your going to have to live with them for a year and it makes for some awkward moments, hiding in the stairs, avoiding them for a while...*
>
> *Rule 102 of halls – don't get too smashed and make a c*nt of yourself...First impressions go a long way especially to the girls. You don't want to be that guy who was sick, passed out in the corner or sh*t in the kettle. Apparently people don't like that...*
>
> Martin Allison

Being homesick

I had been desperate for a long time to move out of the family home, couldn't wait to get down to Glasgow, and had no doubt that's where I wanted to be.

As above, the first few nights had gone well, I had started to make plenty of friends, and when induction week began so did all the spoils of freshers week, and even the course itself seemed like it was going to be alright.

However, rather surprisingly, I was hit by homesickness. I couldn't actually believe it, I thought I would be the last person to feel like that, but for some of that first week I missed home.

It came on suddenly one night. I got a text from a few mates to say they were having a poker night, and were raising a beer to me. All of a sudden I wanted to be home sat round the table with them.

It's hard saying goodbye to friends. And of course, inevitably, you get them all texting you during your first week to ask how things are going.

You're making friends at university, but you've only known them for a few days, of course they're not your best friends yet and you can't completely be yourself in front of them either. Your best friends, the ones that you know best, are three hours up the road and having a poker night without you.

I'd been called Panda since I was at primary school, even some school teachers knew me by my nickname. Yet, I wasn't at home anymore where that was my name and no-one ever had a second thought about it – here I was in Glasgow with people thinking my mum and dad were gypsies who had genuinely named me after a bear.

And that is when you question whether moving halfway round the country is the right idea. Why have you left all your friends behind? Are you going to eventually lose touch with them all?

It can be easy to fold, to bottle it straight away and convince yourself you've made the wrong choice, because you were comfortable at home, you felt safe, and you had friends. Now your room doesn't feel like yours, you like your new friends or flatmates but you're still getting to know them, and your mum and dad are no longer only just down the stairs if you want something.

If you've left a girlfriend or boyfriend back home, well, you can probably multiply all this by ten.

Plenty of students left for home within that first week and never came back.

You'll get over it though if you fight through it. Those new friends will eventually become best friends. That new city where everyone speaks different and is so much bigger and more complicated than what you're used to eventually becomes home. The bedroom that looks like a prison cell eventually does become your cosy wee shack.

Having no-one to do your washing or clean up after you is a nuisance you soon forget, and you will quite enjoy your weekly trips down to the laundry to fight over the machines with everyone else (660 residents, twelve washing machines. Work that one out.)

> **TIP:** *Keep an eye on the timer on the washing machine. You don't need to stand and watch your washing for the 40 minutes it might take, but work out when it's due to finish and make sure you're back five minutes before it's due to end. There's two reasons for this.*
>
> *Firstly, it's a great way to get talking to someone who you might not already know who are impatiently waiting on their washing too.*
>
> *More importantly though, due to the lack of washing machines people tend to empty the machine for you so they can put their own clothes in. Now they might be nice and put it away neatly for you. Others might throw it anywhere. Either way no-one wants their smalls to be on display for everyone to gawp at.*

You'll get into your little routine. Of knowing when to shop and what to shop for, of budgeting your money, of trying to keep the place fairly tidy, or looking after your flatmate when they get sick (or getting Martin to look after her for you).

You'll keep in touch with your mates back home if you really want to. Some I lost touch with, even best mates. Others I still speak to now as often as I ever did.

Put simply, you'll grow up, which is what a big part of university is all about, and you'll relish the challenge of flying the nest.

Best thing to do though is keep your communications with your friends and family to a minimum while you're settling in. Yes, check in; let your parents know you're doing okay, let your mates know you've not forgotten them. However, don't have hour long conversations with your mum or best friend just yet, because you'll come off the phone and feel sad, so you'll miss home that little bit more.

You need to settle in to your new life. It might only take you a few hours, it might take you a few weeks, but you'll do it if you throw yourself into your new life and embrace everything, and then you won't look back.

> *The first few weeks, or even the first three months, is tough if you've moved countries and left family and friends behind. At the start I got really homesick, thought I'd made biggest mistake of my life, but its one of those things that only time can help with.*
>
> *I got over it by throwing myself into student life, spending money I didn't have, drinking so much I couldn't remember what club we went to, burning food, setting off fire alarms when people are in the shower..the usual! After three months it became the best thing I've ever done. Almost five years later I'm still here and loving it more than ever.*
>
> *Gemma Fodey*

Utencils form

You'll get given a form when you move in, asking you to inspect your room and flat for damage, and tick off if everything is okay and mark down anything that is not quite right.

You'll also be asked to check everything you're supposed to have is there, ie bin, cutlery, chopping board, kettle etc.

Very good hint – make sure you fill that in and hand it back to the office. Make sure you are picky and write down every little scratch, mark, or wet patch in your flat.

In second year, when we moved into private halls, we received said form, looked at it, and binned it. The result was we got charged for everything, which landed us a bill for a quite incredible £160.

There was a small plastic bin in my bathroom, which had a slight crack in the lid. I didn't report it because, you know, it's a small plastic bin with a crack in the lid. That small crack cost me £5 to replace at the end of the year.

We got charged for "a damaged chopping board." The damage was knife marks, which generally occur on a chopping board.

A ridiculous £8 bill came our way for a salt and pepper set. A whopping £20 for a pan lid. And so on the bills mounted up, all because by not filling in the form we had accepted the flat was perfect when we moved in, and by acceptance of the terms and conditions, the flat was actually not so perfect, and the management could use that as an excuse to upgrade the flat for the next person at our expense.

So, in short, mention everything, even if you think it'll make you look like a little moaner. And keep your copy of what you filled in. It may save you a few hundred quid at the end of the year.

Also do the same when moving into a flat. Just explain to the landlord why you're doing it, and that you don't expect him to actually go and fix that broken bin lid, you're simply pointing it out now to save any further hassle at the end of your lease. Write everything on a letter, and get your landlord to sign it.

That's for further down the line. You've just moved into halls, met your flatmates, made friends with the flat downstairs, already fancy the girl across the hall, had your wee homesickness fueled breakdown and got over it by reminding yourself you can now do whatever you bloody well like without your parents telling you off.

Aye, this uni malarkey might not be too bad at all. However, we've not even started yet. Next week, is your course induction. Now lets find out what you're really in for.

5
Induction week

This is where it really begins. You've done the meeting and greeting in halls. You can't count how many parties you've been to and how many different people you've met. You're amazed that even with music blaring, people shouting in the corridors, others stumbling home at 4am, people being sick in bins, and all the fun and games of teenagers being given free reign away from home - not once has someone come and told you to behave. This wouldn't happen at home. What would your parents think?

That's just the start. University life really begins for real in freshers week.

It will be a good week of specialised events. How good they are depends on the budget and imagination your new student union has.

The good thing about studying in Glasgow was that there were three universities - one of them had two unions - and armed with a student card you can go to them all.

The events at the other unions may be better (Strathclyde had Oasis and Stone Roses tribute bands playing, we had Eugene from Big Brother 6) but try and go to at least a few nights at your own one because, again, you're trying to make friends, and it's your freshers week – you just have to go.

You also might find your course lecturers put on their own night out too to help you and your classmates get to know each other a little better. We had a little meet and greet in a bar one night that helped us get chatting to classmates and ask the lecturers a bit more about the course. It was a good idea, but they chose a bar that was actually pretty hard to find – especially for us that were new to the city.

Contrary to what you may be led to believe over drunken chats with your new pals - you won't have induction week off just because you're going out every night. You'll be in induction classes for all five days.

We were fortunate in that our course leader was sympathetic to the freshers cause, so he scheduled all our classes that week for the afternoons.

It's a funny few days. At night, all the fresher events are good fun and, let's be honest, it's pretty much the easiest time to go and pull. During the day though the actual timetabled classes are generally boring because everything is one long introduction to your course.

You'll have library introductions which will show you how and where to find books, how to log on to the computers, how to activate and use your e-mail. All very basic stuff but has to be done, and is definitely worth going to.

Attend them, activate your e-mail, learn how to use the online lecture notes facility, find out how you get your exam results - it'll save you a lot of grief later on.

How sober you are for any of these events is up to you, however on day one, class one, it's probably a good idea to be fairly fresh. That 3am drinking session with your new flatmate who arrived on the Sunday might seem like a grand idea at the time, but day one is generally a long day and it's not exactly the one morning you can pull the duvet over you and decide to skip class.

Quite simply, today is the day you will probably be made to meet one of the great fears of man (and woman). Standing up in front of the class of unknowns and introducing yourself.

Now I can't tell you exactly how this will happen, because every course has a different way of doing it, and no doubt every university does too. Some made their students make a mini-presentation, others had to answer questions from the rest of the class, others were simply told to stand up and talk until told to sit down.

Most of us will begin university with at least a tingle of fear at the thought of a room full of strangers all watching you, judging you, and you trying to stutter a few words. They call it character building. That's why, for a lot of your classes, you'll also have to get used to standing up and making oral presentations regularly.

It does serve the purpose that you should complete your degree with the ability to stand up and make presentations at a whim, however we even had a girl on one module faint at the fear of it.

Your first day will go past in a blur, but one thing you will never forget is your first impressions of everyone, and that means they will never forget their first impression of you.

It's something we still laugh about to this day. So make your introduction good.

On day one they sat us down around a load of tables which had been pushed together to make one big square. We all faced each other – every one of us making judgements about people we didn't know. There were only about 20 of us but right away I noticed a heavier ratio of guys to girls. I was sandwiched between one of each – but no way was any of us going to break the ice with a bit of weak small talk.

At one corner there was a group of girls who were talking loudly and laughing. Did they know each other? Had they made friends with each other already?! Why hadn't I sat down there I thought, shit I'm stuck with the anti social losers – wait, I'm one of those anti social losers. Then I scanned the rest of the room. A girl fidgeting awkwardly with her pen. A guy next to her staring at the wall. A guy next to him playing with his phone. There were a group of guys at the other corner. They were talking but it looked like none of them really knew what to say – they hadn't hit it off like the girls at the other side of the room.

At my side no one spoke, we just sat there staring at everyone else and probably all thinking the same thing – where was the teacher? Was this a test? Were they watching us from some two-way mirror to see how we'd interact? I couldn't see any mirrors, and the walls looked pretty normal, but I couldn't help thinking it was some sort of Big Brother style experiment, and at that moment I was failing miserably.

In fact, I'm still convinced to this day it was some sort of set up because about 20 (long, painful) minutes later, the awkward silence, and even more awkward chats, were broken by an extremely convenient fire alarm. Convenient I said? It was horrible. We filed out of the classroom, down the stairs, and gathered on the grassy patch across from the building to re-enact the scene from upstairs. Small talk and silence, trying not to make eye contact with the people you had already decided were a bit strange.

Queuing up to get back into the classroom again I couldn't take the tension anymore. I ended up standing next to the guy who had been sitting next to me so I decided to bite the bullet and break the ice. My eyes zoomed in on the tipex on his black backpack.

"Celtic fan, huh?" I asked, directing my eyes to the 'CFC' graffiti-ed onto his bag. "Yeh." He replied with a smile. And from there it began. A friendship which still lasts to this day.

Laura Brannan

In journalism, we were asked to get into pairs and interview the person next to us. Then, we had to spend two minutes introducing the person to the class. Sound good? No it's not, because now your class' first impression of you relies on what the other muppet is saying, and the girl I partnered with didn't exactly make a good first impression on my behalf.

She didn't actually make it to the first week of university – merely surviving induction week, going home for the weekend with what her flatmates described as a cold, and never returning again.

The poor girl was quite clearly petrified at the thought of speaking to the class. However, she was my partner, I was going to look after her. I'd turn whatever quotes she gave me from the interview into a really good introduction.

So I interviewed her, learned wee things like she was from a small town in the Highlands, had never been to Glasgow before, and was absolutely terrified. That shone through more than anything. Then she interviewed me. When finished we both quietly prepared our speeches, and were ready for our first university challenge.

And so the speeches started. We heard from Steve, who went first and actually impressed with a really good introduction, and had the rest of us frantically scribbling last second edits to our own ones.

We heard from Allan with the ridiculously camp accent, who could talk at a million miles an hour, and I've no idea really what he said. It was supposed to be a two minute speech, he finished his in 30 seconds because he'd talked so quickly.

There was Chris who had moved up from England and had left life in a band behind to become a student. Claire put my three hour trip to shame by revealing she had moved up from London, but had - rather stupidly in my book - side stepped living in halls.

Then, it came to me, with Ken our course leader and messiah nominating my new friend to go first. I sat back and waited for my glowing introduction. It didn't quite work out like that.

Perhaps she actually was a better journalist than I gave her credit for, because she manipulated everything I had said into, well, introducing someone I didn't recognise.

Her best bits were using my throwaway line that "I'm knackered cos of the parties" to "He hates living in halls and living with students. Everyone is too noisy and he can't sleep, and regrets living with young people." Way to make everyone think I'm a boring old git.

Then my line, which was actually in sympathy at the plight of her moving to Glasgow for the first time, that "Yeh Glasgow is a big place" became "He's not sure about Glasgow or Glaswegians", which went down a storm with the half of the class who were all locals. A few gave me the death stare for that, though the ridiculously camp guy had been giving me the death stare since I'd walked in.

Then my line that my favoured area of journalism was sport, was changed to "He doesn't follow politics or current affairs, and only wants to cover sport", which elicited an open mouthed reaction from Ken who nearly jumped out of his seat in outrage. You could see the venom in his face as he thought of the 480 people he had rejected for a place on the course, in favour of a guy who was now revealing he essentially wasn't interested in 90% of what I was meant to be getting taught.

Eventually she finished. A moment of silence before Ken, his eyes glued on mine, said through gritted teeth: "So.......Andrew. What did you think, was it accurate?"

The fact that I had to quickly say "I actually really do like politics" isn't on page one of "how to make other students think you're not a loser."

So it was my turn to introduce her. I looked at my scribbled notes, thought for a second, leaned back and decided to go al fresco.

Now in fairness, I wasn't that bad. I just wanted to get her back. I'm not proud of it, and I'm not even entirely sure of everything I said, but I tried to be funny (which I wasn't) and clever (which again I wasn't).

When the two minutes were up, Ken nodded to my right and asked if my speech was accurate. The poor girl sat stunned, before stammering the classic comment of the day. "Well, I'm not THAT bad."

Oops. Sorry. I hope I had nothing to do with your eventual decision to go home early.

Apart from that though day one was fine. Everyone was quite relaxed. As a bloke, a good icebreaker is always football and it didn't take us long to work out who supported who, and the banter started quite quickly. I can always remember walking out of the room, and being chased down the corridor by a wee guy called Danny spitting "You gave Celtic got a bit of abuse in there did you not?"

Freshers week is one week that you'll grow to love whilst at uni. For the first years, it's basically a great opportunity to see the talent pool, and for everyone else at uni, it's new people that you haven't tried to pull yet.

Normally the student union will put on something every night, this combined with the clubs in the city and the parties in halls make for a crazy few nights. Prepare for several hangovers. Resolve or 'Recovery' from boots becomes a lifesaver. Also be prepared to love fancy dress...pub golf attire, superhero costumes and santa hats are most common.

DON'T get yourself a boyfriend/girlfriend during or before freshers.... you'll miss all the fun.

My freshers week was amazing. It lasted for two weeks as we moved into halls a week before uni started and I genuinely think I was drunk most nights. I swear the guys and girls in my course never saw me fresh until about week two. I put it down to the number of different parties in halls each night and then we all went down to the student union in whatever fancy dress we could find.

Martin Allison

Signing up and getting free stuff

Freshers week brings the freshers fair. These actually change every day. Some days, there will be shops that have brought along gear to sell on the cheap, and you can get that £300 jacket for a fraction of the price. Try not to go too crazy because you're spending valuable drinking money, but if you get there first you do get some cracking discounts.

Others just want to give you free stuff in return for a signature. So go over, give a fake name and e-mail address, and accept your goody bags.

These goody bags are filled with random things. Some times you might get lucky and get perfume or aftershave, others will be just t-shirts, wallets and, inevitably, condoms.

Nightclubs will also be there and you might pick up a free hoody (always try and get one. Winter will hit at some point and being able to throw on a big warm hoody when you're in a rush to get to class is always handy). In addition these clubs will hand out free passes too – grab a handful and treat your mates.

You will also find all the sports clubs and university societies will have their own stalls and will be trying to get you to sign up. Try and join at least one club.

> *A lot can be said for university sports. In my experience it is the best way to meet people and enjoy the time at uni. Most unis have a club for everything and are all desperate for you to join – as they get more funding based on members. However normally there will be some sort of trial/selection process for you to get in but once you are in, you can make a lot of lasting friendships.*
>
> *Some uni's take sports more seriously than others but there is huge emphasis on the social side, it leads to some of my most memorable nights out and the odd game of sport now and then.*
>
> *Wednesdays is sport day and it's essential to do your utmost to keep Wednesday free of classes (if your uni doesn't automatically let you have it off). Being in the football team meant that Wednesday nights were always the highlight, and with that came the sports teams out en masse. Each week there would be several people secretly pulling in Jumping Jacks trying desperately to avoid anyone from sports, others weren't so discreet and were held at "court" the next day to be found guilty for their "crimes". At one point a web of incest between the sports teams was created to show an alarming number of shared connections.*
>
> *We used to play the numbers game when we were out, essentially trying to see who could accumulate the most girls in one night…Points system was as follows:*
>
> *Facebook add: 1 point*
> *Phone Number: 2 points*
> *Kiss: 5 points*
> *Foreplay: 10 points*
> *Sex: 20 points*
>
> *Winner was announced the next day.*
>
> *Martin Allison*

6
Part-time jobs

What do you do when the bank of mum and dad runs dry?

If you're loaded, your parents don't think twice about throwing cash your way, and you don't need to work, then you're a very privileged young man or woman.

However, I would still recommend getting a job.

Obviously, you don't need to work too many hours if you're not bothered about the money, but again it helps improve the social side of things.

Some of my best times at uni were due to working in a nightclub. You're getting into a club for free for a start. You make friends with so many people and the social side is always fantastic. Rather than having to pluck up the courage to approach and talk to the best looking people in the club, they're coming up and approaching you, doing the hard work for you, so you're striking up conversations with all those women (or men) you fancy all night without any effort on your part.

> *Getting a part time job was possibly the best decision...especially in one of Glasgow's biggest clubs! Of course tho I was 18 when I started therefore as you can imagine I loved it. Getting paid to be in a club, WIN!*
>
> *I made friends fast and was in drinking on my nights off making an idiot of myself every night, but I wouldn't change it for the world.*
>
> *Gemma Fodey*

The easiest job to get is working in a bar. Especially a nightclub, as they employ new staff almost every week.

Another job that is easy to come by, and is usually more lucrative money wise, is working as a waiter/waitress due to the tips you get, especially around Christmas time.

At the start of second year, I started working at an Italian restaurant in the city centre. I didn't even consider working there but a girl from back home had just moved to Glasgow, had against my advice shunned halls in favour of a, admittedly, plush flat in the west end, and wasn't the most popular of kids in them first few weeks.

Her mates therefore urged me to introduce her to everyone, which I did, and you'll be happy to know it all worked out well for young Jenna in the end. So much so she even bagged a date with Martin, who by this point had ditched his pursuit of my flatmate, and suggested taking Jenna to the cinema.

There they were taking in a film, them both romantically sat next to each other at the back of the cinema. Our hero quietly looks at his phone and texts his boss to double check what time he starts work. What he thought was a 11pm start was actually an hour earlier. Most men would panic, or at least text their boss an apology and make up some excuse for not being able to make it in on time.

Perhaps, you might even consider a grovelling apology to your date. Not Martin.

He put his phone in his pocket, leaned over and whispered that he was off to work, told her to enjoy the rest of the film, and happily marched out.

I got a call from Martin warning me to expect an angry Jenna in about an hour's time but to tell her he was sorry, and true to form an hour later the phone rang with a raging jilted girl on the other line.

They never had a second date.

> **TIP:** *It's not uncool to make friends with your university lecturer, in fact quite the opposite. You're an adult now, and they will generally treat you as such. There's no more "Mr Garner" or "Mrs McLaughlin". It's Ken and Liz.*
>
> *I found myself out on the town one night drinking when I met two of my lecturers. I ended up getting drunk with them and hearing my assessment marks about two weeks before I was supposed to, and hearing stories that I probably shouldn't have heard.*

So Jenna suggested I join her at the restaurant, and to save me searching for a job I obliged.

Now this was a tough job, because their standards were ridiculous. They had a secret diner once a month, and if anyone was marked below 100%, all the staff had to eat their lunches in the toilet for the next four weeks as punishment. However, the tips were amazing. In fact, in the lead-up to Christmas when they had a lot of work parties in, the tips were nearly double what the wages were.

I eventually left to work with Martin in a nightclub because being an insomniac I used to lie there thinking I should really be getting paid for this time I was awake.

Also, considering the library opening times, I preferred to be free when it was open and to be working when it was shut.

I also liked coming home from uni, having a few hours to myself to make my dinner, put my feet up, maybe grab a quick sleep, then have to worry about going to work.

Others though would rather leave uni, go straight to work while they're alert, be coming home at a reasonable hour and going to bed, then getting up early in the morning and hitting the library or the books then. I prefer to study later in the day, others do it better in the morning.

What's important is to get yourself a routine, especially around exam time. Your uni timetable will dictate much of that, but consider your social life, your sleep, your work and your study into the rest of the week.

> **TIP:** *Always have the number of a trustworthy taxi in your phone. You will need it, either for yourself of a friend. Try and memorise the number should your phone battery run out so you can call from a phone box.*

Another great thing about working in a nightclub is that your social life, rather surprisingly considering your hours, increase.

Nightclub staff are, mostly, students. Of course, students do what students do best, they organise plenty of nights out.

When I was a waiter, most of the staff - as friendly as they were - were foreigners who had come here to work. Most of their wages were going back home to poor family members. And so, apart from the Christmas night out, the social scene wasn't up to much.

I might mention the "social scene" a bit much in this book, but I'm not trying to turn you into a mad party animal.

If you're committed to your course then you'll do enough work. It's important to have friends so you can enjoy life away from the ring too.

> *During my degree I tried to juggle too many shifts with my studies and it ended up having a detrimental effect on my grades. I was missing lectures so that I could do extra shifts so that I could save up for a holiday with my mates to Magaluf in the summer.*
>
> *The holiday was certainly worth it but failing my first degree wasn't ideal. A part-time job is a great thing to have, it allows you extra money to have a social aspect to uni (very important, don't just be stuck in books everyday) but be sensible and only do a couple of shifts a week.*
>
> *Daniel Hayes*

Of course there's another choice, in retail. Thing about that is, you get no tips. I'd only have done retail at university if it was in a clothes shop, but by all accounts the interviews are generally group ones, and notoriously hard. You need to be very fashion conscious and I'm told by people who went to these interviews that you should be prepared to talk about the store, the sort of clothes they have, and maybe the sort of style you like to wear. Don't go in saying you're skint and you need the money.

Do it for the clothes discount I suppose.

That said working in a phone shop isn't bad, because you get commission on what you sell, and once you're past your probation period you'll probably find a very healthy discount on your mobile phone contract too.

Again though, the interviews are hard. A typical application for EE for example is an online test, a phone interview, an hour long interview in person that includes a ten minute presentation and two role playing exercises, and then a four day induction that could be at the other end of the country.

You'll probably find it's a great thing to have on the CV though, and if it's a big company then it's possibly a good start for you on the career ladder. Start low at Mark's and Spencers, do a degree in marketing, business or fashion, and work your way up.

Generally, people didn't think that far ahead. It was either waiting staff or bar person for most people I knew. But there's a range of choices – others I know even got jobs in call centres, and of course working as a PR is easy work, as is handing out leaflets, but in Scotland it can get a bit cold.

I do think there is an expectation that when you go to uni you should be having one night stands all the time. I barely know anyone who did this, if anything most people met their boyfriends and girlfriends at uni.

I did have one one night stand, it was terrible! I couldn't remember his name and I ended up at a very small party with him two years later where I couldn't avoid him, and of course it all got brought up and was incredibly awkward. Still, I'm glad I did it, it's something to tick off my bucket list!

What I would say though, is having your own flat often results in hoards of people from back home staying over, and this resulted in a lot of sleeping with our friends. So it is a great time for sexual experimentation for a lot of people, and is how I met my husband.

Natalie Monty

A summer abroad

Of course one place where it's not cold is Ayia Napa, Cyprus. One summer I went to work there for four months. The money is horrible but you're not there to top up your pension.

I would definitely recommend doing it at least once. If not Cyprus then Ibiza, Crete, Corfu, or wherever takes your fancy. If you can get away with doing it every summer you're at uni then go for it.

It can be brilliant, but there are a lot of things to be wary of too.

Firstly, the best time to go is in May. The bars and clubs will have been open for a few weeks, and are just starting to get busy enough to need some staff.

I went early June and was lucky to get a job. It seemed to be the only job left to be honest; and after that every day we were bombarded with people asking for work, any work, because there was nothing going.

If you can't make it end of May, then towards the end of June or the beginning of July more jobs become available because it's approaching high season so everywhere needs more staff. It's still competitive though.

The only time it's not competitive is around September because a lot of workers start flying home – either because they're homesick, have ran out of money, or they are students and need to get back to re-start their course. You can take your pick of the jobs then. Don't expect it to be much fun around that time though, that's generally when you think of going home and it tends to be mainly families milling about.

Don't bother signing up with some agency before you leave, who will promise you a job. I never knew anyone who got a job with them, and you're paying money up front with no guarantee of getting paid employment.

You get a job by going on holiday for a week, scouting the best bars, chatting to the owners and bar staff and making friends, and then asking about jobs. If he or she likes you then they might give you a job there and then. Or, they might at least let you know of a job going somewhere else and tell you the bosses to avoid working for.

They want people who are friendly and chatty. They also want someone they can trust. Most bars will let you have a few drinks while you're working and it wasn't uncommon to finish your shift already drunk. However don't cross the line, and **don't** whatever you do try to be sly and pocket money or steal from the owner. I saw people dragged out and punched on the street by bar owners, because they thought someone had pocketed money instead of putting it in the till.

If you don't turn up for a shift you can also consider yourself sacked. If the owner owes you any money then you won't see it. It's not like here where you've signed a contract – it's cash in hand over there and they'll shrug their shoulders and tell you to get out when they feel like it.

At my "interview" if you can call it that, the bar owner poured me a pint, sat me down at a table, looked at me and said in a Greek/Cypriot accent "If you fuck me, I fuck you more".

Sometimes it's all a bit unfair and I remember one waitress getting sacked and accused of stealing, and she swore she didn't take anything and I believe her because she didn't need the money – her tips jar was already overflowing every night.

However she was thrown out with the bar owner shouting "You're lucky you are a girl." I think you can work out what that means.

Some places only pay you monthly. Try and avoid them as

without a contract you're essentially at their mercy, and if you fall out with your boss and get sacked they'll keep all your money, even hundreds of pounds.

Try to find places that pay nightly. You might get a place that keeps your first three nights wages as security and only give you it back when you leave, but that's fine. Losing three nights wages is preferable to losing a month's.

I got a job as barman in a Scottish bar because when the boss said there were no jobs going I kept on talking, trying to convince him to let me know if a vacancy came up. I think he also liked the fact I was Scottish so would be able to understand what half the customers were on about. He phoned me up a day later, said he'd sacked his barman, and to come in.

I got my second job, as a PR, by getting drunk, cheekily asking the boss in a Pirate's themed bar about the job advertised outside, being invited into the back for a quick chat, and told to start there and then. I told him I was drunk, he said "Good, I won't have to give you any free drink to get you drunk then" and five minutes later I was dressed a pirate working as a PR on the streets. That's life in Ayia Napa.

It's easy going but there are a lot of horrible bosses over there too. Also be careful round the bouncers, I lost count of the amount of times I'd see some poor kid get a leathering from a group of doormen who were basically just paid thugs.

Generally, book yourself a hotel for two weeks, then ask about for worker's accommodation. People in the know will recommend good ones and maybe even offer to share with you. Don't just go and grab the first place you find and end up being ripped off. You may also get a special discount in a hotel if you sign up for the whole summer – they'll let you stay there for cheaper than normal as it's better than having an empty room.

Most of the worker's accommodation are absolute holes though, and you'll be sharing a room with two or three people. Try and find somewhere safe to stores your valuables, and don't carry too much money on you.

As for what jobs to do, bar staff is the obvious one. It's a tough job to get though because most bar owners prefer to employ locals.

However, generally theme places (ie I worked in a Scottish bar so having a Scottish barman made sense) will employ non-locals. It's hard graft, you'll be really busy especially in high season, and I worked long hours without a single day off. The money is better than other jobs over there though and you can top it up with tips, but it's still less than the minimum wage back here. Also if you think a boss is worried about being able to trust a PR or waitress, think how paranoid he gets over a barman.

It was a strange job. I remember being told to turn up at 6pm on my first day. A Romanian barman, with cigarette in his mouth, gave me a quick tour of the bar. "Press this to open the till. This is the price of beer. That's the cocktail menu, try and learn it before it gets busy." I wasn't really paying too much attention because I just thought I'd pick everything up from him as I went along.

Of course he then says "Okay, Savvas (the boss) will be in at 9pm. Good luck," and he walked out! I was left alone in charge of a bar I'd literally been working in for two minutes, in a country I'd been in for two days, and I had to run the whole place by myself for three hours.

For a boss who was so paranoid about everything I'm amazed he did that, but every night I was essentially the manager for three hours every day. I even got to decide what staff to employ if we were short of a waitress. I'd tell the ugly girls the job had been taken, and only let the good looking ones know it was still available!

It was a tough slog every night, especially when the resort got busier and the weather got hotter – even at night it was too hot for a t-shirt – but we had some of the best staff in that place. The bar staff, the PRs, waitresses and DJs all partied together and went to the same clubs after work.

We'd finish at 1.30am, hit the clubs until 4am, then head to the after-party clubs that went on until 7am. Sometimes we'd even head to the beach, or one of the 24 hour bars at someone's hotel, and carry on the drinking until lunchtime. Then it was home to catch up on any sleep I could get, try grab some food, and I was back at work at 6pm again ready for another mad night.

I did that every night for two months until I couldn't take any more. I hadn't had a single day off, it was busy, it was hot, I was hungover most nights, I wasn't getting enough sleep because even if you vowed to go home straight after work someone would entice you out, and half the time I was starving too because I'd wake up in a rush to get to work and wouldn't have time to eat.

I barely got a suntan because the only time I saw daylight was walking home in the morning from a night out.

I kept trying to quit and my boss kept offering me a pay rise to stay! In the end I was probably one of the highest paid staff in Ayia Napa, but after two months I finally quit and became a PR at another bar for the next two months. I wished I'd done it the other way around and been PR in the months it was busy, and barman later in the season when it was quiet.

Promotion staff, or PRs, is probably the best job to get. You get drunk, you chat up people on the street, and you try and get them into your club or bar. Some places give you tickets and actually keep a note of how many people you get in, which means you're actually competing with your fellow staff members. Others you're working as a team. Get the team ones, they're the best laugh and means you can banter away with the other PRs without fighting over customers.

Like I said above, I did it the wrong way around. I was a PR when it started to get quiet and most of the young party-goers were replaced by families who were not as interested in being enticed into the bars for shots and cocktail buckets.

The money is generally 20 – 25 euros a night, and you can barely cover the cost of your accommodation and food, and you might even be struggling to raise the cash to book the eventual flight home, so only do this if you've got a bit of money in the bank already.

It might sound easy, and when the streets are mobbed and your bar already has a good reputation so people are making a beeline for it then yes, it's the best job to have. Your boss lets you drink all night because they want you in the party spirit to give the impression everyone in your place is having a great time.

When it gets quiet and you're competing with other bars, your voice is going and you're getting no banter off anyone, and you can't be bothered to be original anymore so just repeat "You coming in for a drink?" over and over, then it's a little less fun.

Prepare for a lot of rejection, you'll need a thick skin. Some people hated us. They were on holiday to enjoy themselves and we were the enemy badgering them. PRs serve a purpose though, because when you're on holiday you don't actually realise if you walk into a bar or club without speaking to a PR you're paying far more for your drinks. The PR is there to offer you deals to get you in. One advice I always gave people was never walk into a bar without finding the PR first.

You might be annoyed at having a dozen of them approach you in the street asking you how you're getting on, where you're going, why don't you come in here for a drink. However they've maybe been there for four hours being told to f**k off by everyone, while an angry boss is storming out to shout at them because the bar isn't busy enough. Just a "Maybe later" will do it.

Any job over there is hard to be honest, and you get rubbish money because there are more people looking for jobs than there is roles available. You've just got to remember though it's a few hours work and then you've the rest of the time to enjoy a four month long stay in a holiday resort.

For girls, the best paying job is waitress, ferrying drinks from the bars to holidaymakers. Guys might get a job as a waiter in a restaurant, but in bars it's usually waitresses only. The pay is rubbish but the tips are phenomenal, and the tips are good for a reason.

Here's the thing. There's no point in going if you're a bit of a prude. As sleazy as it sounds, the bar owners want hot women working for them, who are happy to wear skimpy outfits, show off their cleavage, midriff and legs, and flirt with the customers. If a group of lads fancy you, they'll stay in the bar drinking all night, and spend most of their holiday in there trying to pull you.

Even I was told at quiet times to go flirt with a group of girls, or make friends with a group of lads my own age who I could chat away about football with. If someone came in from Aberdeen, I was told to go over to their table with some free shots, tell them it was from me, and chat away about the Dons.

So, be prepared to be a big flirt and maybe a little slutty if you're a girl, and even if you're a guy! Prepare to be given a staff t-shirt and then told to get a pair of scissors and cut it so it leaves little to the imagination. The money they made from tips was worth it, and you never saw any of them having to buy a drink in the clubs either (which is free entry to staff, and generally there's a workers bar so you get served quicker too, and usually armed with drinks vouchers).

In reality, if you're a good looking girl then you can pretty much pick your job and actually make yourself a bit of money. You ladies have it made. A bar that gets a reputation for having the best looking staff will get mobbed.

There are probably better jobs out there of course. If you can get your hands on something going at a hotel as receptionist, then you may find your pay and hours are much better but I didn't meet many receptionists on a night out, so I presume the social side wasn't as good.

There are those who work as DJs. A lot of the bars are karaoke, so you'll need to do plenty of singing. You'll usually have to organise them jobs through a company most of the time, and be prepared to stay for the full season (March to November in some cases) which isn't handy if you're a student, unless you get there early and approach a bar owner and tell him you'll do it for half the price.

There are of course jobs going as holiday reps too, but these are actual jobs and not ones you can quit early or start late because you've to get back to university, or are homesick.

Overall, it's a great experience. You have to deal with tough bosses, and sometimes the locals see you as easy prey to pickpocket, but just be sensible about things. Most of the above was just to warn you about the downsides of working abroad. I loved my four months in Ayia Napa. I loved the nightlife, and I loved it even more knowing I was enjoying it for far cheaper than people on holiday were due to the generous worker's discounts. I loved the weather (what I saw of it), fellow workers, and sometimes being behind the bar or out on the streets chatting up a big group of girls was brilliant fun.

Prepare to work hard for little money; just like university really. Again though, do it right and you'll have the time of your life.

7
Flatmates

If there's one thing you can't prepare for, it's flatmates. Even if you have experience of living with flatmates before, every person is unique, and therefore every set of flatmates is unique.

I left for uni in 2005. In the next five years (two spells) I'd have a whopping 25 flatmates. 25! That doesn't even count people I stayed with after I graduated.

First year brought me together with the range of characters introduced in chapter four, but what a year it was in university halls and still my best year of uni.

Second year was a better flat in that I had chosen my flatmates so I knew what to expect, and the accommodation was slightly better as we'd chosen private halls.

Third year was bizarre. It started with what I though was every man's dream; living with three girls. That dream turned into a nightmare when I thought I was going to be stabbed to death one night (I'll tell that story later).

> *In second year, myself and my best mate rented a house that didn't have any working central heating and the landlord just didn't care. Most nights we'd make cups of tea and not drink them, just hold them to keep warm! The house was a nightmare but we still had good fun. There was a fire but the panels on the front kept coming off, and we tried to stick them back on but when the fire was lit it melted the glue and the fumes nearly made us collapse. Also halfway through the year the roof in the bathroom fell in!*
>
> *Anyway, in our final year, we rented a much better place in Belfast, with a Vicar as a Landlord. The place was spotless and warm and much better kept. So my advice is, always get a man of the cloth as a landlord.*
>
> *Colin Robertson*

Choosing your flatmates

Towards the end of first year, everyone in halls will have formed their own groups, and you'll be looking for flatmates.

Some universities will let you stay in halls for second year – some in fact have halls specifically for second years.

It will never be as good as first year so don't expect it to be, but if you've chosen your flatmates then don't rule it out.

Four of us chose private halls for second year, two boys and two girls. We knew each other so that was good, and most halls are located near your university so it was walking distance for us, in fact across the road from where we'd been living the previous year.

The price was maybe a bit more expensive than renting a flat, but it was safe, clean, every room was en-suite, and it saved us the hassle of searching round the city for somewhere to stay and having to deal with landlords.

Bear in mind though all halls are noisy. Even if there are no parties - doors bang, people shout in the lift, and worst of all – the fire alarm goes off constantly.

You will never get used to being woken up when in a deep sleep, having to get out of your bed and stand in the cold outside for 45 minutes, and wait while the fire brigade give the all clear.

All this due to someone burning their toast. And this happens at least once a week.

Of course, for that reason you may consider a flat is better, then find your flatmates are still party animals.

Myself and one flatmate spent most of second year working in a nightclub, so we would be coming in regularly at 4 – 4.30am, which I don't think the two girls appreciated.

Likewise, they both had placements as part of their course and would often rise at 7am when we were trying to get some much needed sleep, so it worked both ways.

Consider who you're living with. Two of my flatmates actually fell out because one was tidy and the other was too messy for their liking.

They had lived together in first year without any problems but one I think just got fed up of it by second year.

> *In one flat my kitchen sink became a public health hazard. It was a flat in China town where my flat was the only non-Chinese household and we were the lowest flat in the building (bins were under us).*
>
> *In short there was a plumbing incident which meant that every time any of the flats above me (as well as my own flat) emptied their sinks, baths or flushed their toilets the waste would back up through my kitchen sink. It turned out this was caused due to the local love of fish cuisine, the wasted oil from such a cuisine had been poured by all the flats above me down their kitchen sinks and had blocked up the local waste water pipes in the surrounding area. It was blocked to such an extent it took the council three days to sort.*
>
> *That's right, for three days and nights I had to bail the local waste water out of my kitchen sink using a kitchen pot three times an hour, and base my toilet breaks into the uni opening times and 'showered' in the uni toilet sinks.*
>
> *Craig Forson*

Also important. In fact very important. Don't ever move in with a girl or boy who you fancy.

You might think that getting the chance to live with them is a dream come true, but it isn't. From speaking to many people, they all say the same – never rent from (or rent to) a hot girl or boy, because you don't want to fall in love with them.

Living with someone puts you into the friend zone, because who wants to date someone they're living with knowing if it doesn't work out you will still see each other every day?

There's only two things that will happen. You will either get it on with the object of your desire, and it will lead to an awkward flat for either you or your other flatmates if it doesn't work out long term.

Or, more likely, you won't get anywhere with them, and it will be a nightmare. You will have to watch when they parade their boyfriend/girlfriend around the flat for the best part of a year, or listen to them coming back after a date.

If you make a move on someone in a nightclub and get rejected, you leave them alone. Make a move on your flatmate – one of you is moving out.

Imagine sitting in the living room one night, just you and your flatmate, and you're having a really good night. You're flirting away, both laughing your heads off, even have managed to move the conversation onto really personal and even sexual topics.

You think you're finally making a connection. You can feel it, you sense she can feel it. Maybe she's having second thoughts about you being in just the friend zone.

Then the doorbell rings, and it's her boyfriend who has made a surprise visit. She's not even that happy to see him, but he's here now, and they head upstairs, and you know, and he knows, and she knows, that they haven't gone up there to proofread her latest university essay. So you phone everyone trying to find someone who will go for a pint with you so you can get out of the house.

It's not worth it. Trust me. Just get a separate flat.

A better idea would be to move in next door to them, not actually with them. You're close enough to see them every day if you need to, but if it doesn't work out you can avoid each other quite easily.

Likewise, don't move in with a couple. They'll spend all their time together and be boring flatmates.

If you're a boy, don't move in with a flat of girls. You might think it's heaven and that they are going to be really tidy, the flat will smell nice, they'll run around after you, and you'll be the godfather of the house with your little harem.

It's not like that at all. Girls like staying in their bedrooms. I lived with three girls in first year who stayed in their rooms, two girls in second year who stayed in their rooms, and three girls in third year who....you get the picture.

Girls stay in their room. Lads come through and watch the football with you. Stay with guys, and have girls as your next door neighbours.

Looking back I can confidently say I have no real regrets. Yes if put in the same situations again I would have done things differently but hey its part of growing up. I was there between 17-21 so I was not only doing a degree but also becoming an adult and learning about who I was as a person. Part of that is making mistakes, saying the wrong thing to the wrong person, and the inevitable financial breakdown.

Craig Forson

In third year, I moved into a flat. Actually, two flats over the course of that year it turned out. Here's some of the problems encountered.

- **What to do if someone moves out of a flat you are renting from a landlord.**

Check your contract carefully before signing it, and get someone in the know to read it over.

We had one flatmate who had never lived away from home before say she was homesick and move out. That led to our landlord demanding we found a replacement or we would have to cover the cost of her room.

In most cases that shouldn't be an issue, and you will rent by the room even if you are renting as a group, but always check. If someone is moving out early speak to the landlord sharpish, and they will usually let you find a replacement, but if you can't then of course you will have to accept they will move someone of their choosing into that room. Even a maniac wielding a knife.

When we all eventually moved out before the end of the contract (the first girl had already moved out, the rest of us left before Christmas) we were told that according to the contract, moving out early breached the agreed terms because we were meant to be there for 12 months, and therefore even if we found new flatmates to move in we were not entitled to our deposit back. Crucially, none of us even had a copy of the contract, which was another major error.

At the time we didn't challenge it, because we had signed a contract and it was the first one we'd ever had in a flat, so we were all a bit wet behind the ears. However there are laws – in Scotland at least – that protect you. A landlord is now under obligation to pay your deposit to a third party (called a "Tenancy Deposit Scheme") where they will have to give a suitable reason for you not being returned your deposit.

You can read more about it here:
http://www.scotland.gov.uk/Topics/Built-Environment/Housing/privaterent/government/SGTD1

> *TIP: When working on an essay, back up everything three times. Save it to the computer, save it on a USB pen, and also e-mail it to yourself. Do this for everything.*

When looking for a flat to rent, you'll find it can be harder work than you think. There can be a lot of competition, and you'll rarely be the only one viewing that flat. The more interest, the higher the landlord will feel he can charge.

Always try and find friends who are already in a flat, and find when they plan to move out. It can be handy if, when they are approaching the end of their contract, they tell the landlord you're looking to move in straight after them. That worked for one of the flats we moved into when three girls moved out, allowing us three lads to snap it up a month later. The landlord was happy to not have to advertise it and give viewings. It also worked for us in that he kept the rent at roughly the same cheap levels the girls were getting, which was a lot, LOT cheaper than our neighbours were paying.

When you view a flat, ask to see the last few bills for it. They might simply tell you the cost, but ask nicely to see a written bill. We found the electric/gas bills were extortionate in our first flat. Perhaps there was a fault, or the property simply used up a lot of electric and gas, but we suffered some extremely high bills after being promised the average cost would be much lower. If the landlord won't let you actually view a copy of a recent bill, then don't move in. Even if the rent seems cheap it will work out more expensive in the end if the bills are high.

Also, check for any extra costs. Your flat might have "factor fees", which if you live in a block of flats will be an extra cost shared between all the tenants to cover stair cleaning, corridor lighting, lift maintenance or gardening. You may even have to pay if you have a private parking space.

In addition to this, you need to know how these bills will be charged. Are they in your landlord's name, or are they being put in your name?

Work out a system early with your flatmates how you'll pay your rent and bills. Sometimes one of your flatmates will be on the lease rather than all of you. If that flatmate is you, then you're liable for the rent, so make sure your flatmates all have standing orders set-up to transfer the money to you on the day the rent is due, or preferably the day before. Don't ever rely on a flatmate doing it by memory.

A better idea is to set-up a separate bank account. Have at least two signatories on it, pay all your rent money in, and then set a standing order up from that directly to your landlord. Therefore if someone defaults on their payment, it is not your personal bank account that suffers.

You can also pay your bills from that extra account – perhaps everyone chipping in a certain amount a month. Aim to pay a bit more than you need to so you cover yourself, and then at the end of the year if there is money left you can close the account and split the extra cash.

If you're a full-time student, you don't have to pay council tax. It's important to know this should you move in with people who aren't students, as they might ask you to split the cost of council tax with them. That's up to you if you want to do that or not, but you'll be paying money you shouldn't have to.

There are slightly illegal ways for a non-student to get off with council tax if he or she is living with students. I couldn't possibly put them in a family book. On a completely unrelated note though isn't google a brilliant thing? Try and think of some things you could type into google and see what results and advice come up.

In second year, I moved into a flat with two other girls and two boys. It was a big flat but had no living room. I had the smallest bedroom by a long way which we all argued about (and I gave in earliest). The place was a dump but we didn't treat it well either. One night one of the guys couldn't get his key to work in the door (drunk) so he kicked it in. We waited about six weeks before a new lock was added so just left all our stuff and slept with a door stop against the door.

The flat was dirty pretty quickly. We didn't have a cleaning rota but each had a room to look after and one guy was on bin duty. It all broke down after a few weeks. No one was cleaning so the 'bin boy' went on strike. I think at one point there were eight full bin bags sitting in the hall which nobody could be bothered to move for a few weeks.

Laurann De Verteuil

So, aye. That time I nearly got stabbed....

Towards the end of second year, we all started thinking about where we were going to live over summer and into third year. I had done two years of halls, and the general feeling amongst everyone was that it was probably time to now move into a flat.

One of the girls I was already living with, Sarah, suggested I move in with her. She had found a four bedroom house in the Merchant City area of Glasgow, where the rent was well within everyone's budget. Currently they only had three girls to fill it, they needed a man to look after them all.

When you hear three girls want you to live with them, you don't think it over, you say yes. Of course you do.

Looking back, I should have politely said no, but I didn't. You already know how the story goes.

That wasn't the only disaster of a flat that I'm sure was cursed.

The bills were extortionate. I wouldn't have been surprised to learn there was a fault with the meter, because our bills were far more than they should have been.

Another one of Sarah's friends had moved in with us but then decided - without telling us - that she was moving out.

We were only given that news when the landlord phoned to ask if we had found a replacement flatmate, because if we didn't we would be charged for her room.

I phoned the girl's dad to try (politely) to resolve the situation, as we did feel, rightly, that it should be her bill and not ours. A polite phone call quickly descended into Tom Cruise's epic "Show me the money" scene in Jerry Maguire.

Actually it didn't, it was more like Tom Cruise in a few good men when Demi Moore has suggested the impossible, and I sat there while her mad father tore me apart for daring to suggest his daughter moving out and not telling us, and leaving us with a bill for her room, was bad manners.

I got blamed for her being homesick. I got blamed for the landlord deciding to charge for the room. I got blamed for Scotland's failure to qualify for any World Cup since France 1998.

With the bills mounting, and increasingly strained relationship with the landlord, we decided to move out and go our separate ways.

The two remaining girls found their own place in December, and I lined up my friends flat that three girls I knew were moving out of for me and two other mates to move into in January.

That meant I had a month alone in the flat before moving out, but the landlord moved swiftly to fill up the rooms with three random flatmates he had found himself, which was his right of course. It was better than him charging me for all four rooms I suppose.

Now, I need to tell the rest of this story with names, I can't keep saying "flatmate one" etc. However, to protect the guilty, and to save any of these angry stars of the story coming back for a second chapter, I feel this story should also be told with names changed..

So, let's call flatmate one Rob, a security man from England.

Let's call the second boy Niall, a call centre worker, and Emma, a fellow student who was from the USA.

The names are the only untrue parts of this story – everything else genuinely happened.

Now Rob was a strange one. He never ate, and kept himself awake by doing drugs; speed normally, but there was a fair bit of cocaine going round the flat too.

Going by the state of some of his friends - who would come to the door shaking with a cold, dead look in their eyes - I'm sure he was on much harder stuff as well, but that's just me speculating.

He wasn't healthy, that much was certain, and he suffered mood swings.

At times he came across as vulnerable and even quite likeable. At other times he would march round the house paranoid and angry, demanding to know who had stole his money, his cigarettes, or why we were all laughing at him behind his back. He wasn't a particularly great guy to live with.

I also had to put up with people turning up at the door looking for drugs. I came home from work one night, at 4.30am, to find a girl so absolutely spaced out on drugs she could hardly move or talk.

I walked into the flat to find her in my living room, shaking and slurring her speech, smelling of all sorts, asking for Rob and, bizarrely, her hat.

She had been let in by a friend of Emma's, who was in bed unconcerned about the whole thing. Her friend actually stopped me at the door as I was opening it and asked "Who are you?".

Yes, question the man walking in with his own keys, but let the foul smelling women who doesn't quite know what planet she's on to stride in and make herself at home.

She asked for Rob – who wasn't even in. I think I'm quite a polite fellow, and I would normally hate the thought of kicking a girl out onto the street, and it didn't actually sit well with me doing that, but this just wasn't right and at that time of the morning I just wanted it to be someone else's problem.

I told Rob about it the next day. His eyes suddenly widened like I'd just announced North Korea were attacking us, and he said: "Don't let her in, don't let her in again. If she comes round again, don't let her in."

Aye, I think me inviting her in was the least of your worries there pal.

Other nights random girls, who rather than being drop dead gorgeous just looked pale and ready to actually drop dead, would leave Rob's drug den and invite themselves into my bedroom. I had to shoo them out of the room before I caught anything.

One day I had the neighbours come to the house to complain about the noise they had experienced in previous evenings - nights I'd been at work where unbeknown to me "Junkies have been trying to kick your door in at 3am".

Try having that conversation with an angry husband and wife, on your doorstep, when you've had three hours sleep, and are hearing that junkies regularly turn up at your front door. It's a lot of fun. Not in the slightest bit worrying.

Any sane person at that point would have phoned the landlord and had them deal with it.

I didn't, I was moving out in a matter of weeks so I just shrugged my shoulders and got on with it. I mean, what's the worst that could happen?

Well......

One night, on a rare weekend night off, the three flatmates were out drinking together. I had been invited out with them, but chose to go out instead with one of the two girls I used to live with, Sarah.

Being a lightweight she got absolutely plastered on a couple of shots of Apple Sourz, so I'd taken her home, which was a trial in itself.

I got her back to her flat, thought I'd be a good friend and attempt to put her to bed, but she managed to roll off and hit her head on a wooden panel. When I lifted her back up she had a sizeable lump growing.

She was drunk, I was fairly sober, but she was a nurse and therefore the one with the medical knowledge, so when she told me she was concussed I took her word for it.

So there I was, sat for an hour with a bag of frozen pees held to her head, while she talked the sort of drunken rubbish girls do when they've had a few too many glasses of pop.

When I was happy all was well she was finally put to bed, I told her to call me in the morning, and off home I went to my empty flat.

I sat down, and took my shoes off, and relaxed. Quick drink, a slice of toast, short game of the X-box and then I'd go to bed.

Then BOOM!! All of a sudden there was a thunderous noise, followed by every object in the kitchen shaking. Before I could even work out what was happening another one hit. Maybe North Korea were attacking after all.

It soon dawned on me, it was the unmistakable sound of someone trying to kick my front door in.

Now not to get all Kevin Bridges on you, but when you're living in Glasgow not far from the East End, it's past midnight, and someone is trying to kick your front door in........well, you get a tad nervous.

Is it the police raiding the place? Is it a drug dealer looking for Rob? Is it one of his nutjob friends looking to get in?

It was like a horror movie. Should I hide? Should I try escape somehow? Should I find something to fight them with?

I was trying to find anything I could swing at them. I picked up the X-box controller, preparing myself to launch it when they came storming into the room. Aye, that's right, I'm armed with an X-box controller and I'm not scared to use it.

You could just imagine three hooded men breaking into the house, roaring into the living room armed with baseball bats ready to trash the house and to take my head off, only to by met by me stood holding an X-box controller. I'm confident the three of them would have slowly backed away while one of them whispered "You said he wouldn't be armed".

As it goes, Glasgow's drug gangs were preoccupied that night, and it was actually Rob who came flying through the door, managing to boot it open after a wee struggle.

Proud of his hard fought victory, he strode into the living room, planted himself on the sofa, and explained – in the event that I maybe had been too engrossed in something else and missed the contest - he'd "Just kicked the door in."

Yes, I gathered that mate by the not hard to distinguish sound of you putting your boot through it. Why would you kick your own door in?

"Lost me keys, innit".

Then ring the doorbell you bloody idiot!

Shortly after, in walked the other two, who then proceeded to berate the hapless Rob for his behaviour in the pub.

The story emerged that a young couple in the bar were celebrating getting engaged that night. Rob saw it as an invitation to chat the girl up, not put off by the fact she's just told the love of her life she'll marry him.

When unsurprisingly to all except Rob she rebuffed the approach, he decided to launch a tirade of abuse at her, and had even thrown a bottle at the groom to be.

Rob was getting it in the neck from Emma, and as this argument went on, myself and Niall had decided to have a short game of FIFA, putting the controllers to better use rather than as potentially lethal weapons.

This reasonable conversation went on for a bit, with Emma telling him he needed to grow up, get off the drugs, and sort his life out. It seemed to be going well until the point Emma had her hands round his neck screaming "I could fucking kill you."

You know what, she probably could have. She was a big girl. I mean she was built. She was living with three lads but she could have broke any of us in half if she wanted.

Rob, with her hands round his neck, shouted at her "Why don't you kill me then", shrugged her off and headed over to the kitchen area which was within the living room, and grabbed a knife.

He threw it at her, and it bounced off her leg and landed beside her.

Emma looked down, stoney faced, while she pondered the thought: "He just threw a knife at me and asked me to kill him. Should I take him up on that offer?"

Before she could react Niall reached over and grabbed the

weapon, handed it to me, and I hid it safely under the cushion.

Rob bounded over and demanded it. I was laughing. He wasn't. What was going on here? I told him to sit down. He ignored me and again demanded the knife.

I saw a look in his eyes that I never want to see again. A look I can only describe as eyes staring at me but seeing something else – probably the face of that scary clown on the Saw films.

I gulped, expecting him to pounce on me and start a wrestle for the knife. Instead he replied "Fine, I'll get a bigger knife then."

Niall and I looked at Emma, whose demeanour was worryingly heading south. Her fist started to clench, her breathing became more controlled. If Rob threw another knife at her, she was going to react like a bear being whipped.

Rob reached into the draw, and pulled out a butcher's knife. He threw it, and the point jabbed Emma's thigh. "Come on then," he shouted. "Kill me."

I don't know if the jab hurt as it poked her leg, but this time there was no chance for Niall to react first and grab the blade. Emma jumped up, with knife in hand, and went for Rob.

Niall leapt across the room at Emma trying to stop her. Now, he wasn't exactly a skinny bloke. He wasn't a big guy, but he looked like he could handle himself. That counted for little, for the poor guy put every effort he had into trying to wrestle with this massive yank and get the knife off her.

I swear he was on her back at one point trying to hold her back, and she just threw him round the room like a ragdoll. It was like watching someone trying to hang on to a Bucking Bronco.

Me? Well I continued my game of Fifa. It was tough, but two goals in the dying minutes of the game earned me a solid 2-0 win. I switched the computer off, finished my drink, wished everyone good night and went to bed.

At least I wished that's what had happened. I wanted to be anywhere but in that room at that time, but I had little choice, so I reluctantly got myself involved.

I ran over to Rob, trying desperately to drag him out of the room in an effort to stop the place becoming a murder scene. He kept trying to get closer to Emma so she could actually stab him, while screaming at her to "do it, fucking kill me."

I could get him as far as the door. I had to let go with one hand though to actually open it, and you can't hold someone back with just one arm, and so back we'd go towards a huge knife wielding American.

Sometimes the blade would swing past precarious parts of my body, other times Rob would surge towards Emma and nearly push me onto the sharp blade.

I'm not going to lie kids, I wasn't exactly thinking at the time "Nice one, this will be a good story to tell my pals tomorrow. Oh how we'll all laugh one day at this." I was expecting someone else to be writing about it in a newspaper with a quote appealing for witnesses to my death.

"I'm phoning the police" I shouted, rather pathetically. It had no effect apart from a shout back "good, do it." Er, alright then.

Of course I couldn't. In the time it would have taken me to let go of the mad suicidal idiot, pick up the phone and call the police, that knife could have been sticking out of someone.

Truth be told, I would happily have let Emma and Rob kill each other, but I owed it to Niall to try and stop the carnage otherwise he may have ended up being the victim.

Plus, perhaps paranoia had taken hold, but I couldn't help but think if someone is in that much of a rage that they're willing to stab someone else, or even have someone stab you, then once you've sliced one person apart would you not just take care of everyone else in the room?

So, we struggled on. I don't know how long for. I can't even remember what happened because eventually the adrenaline kicks in when you're in a situation like that, and you go from trying to be the good guy calming everything down, to losing it with the fella who's nearly got you killed three times in the last thirty seconds.

Did I punch him? Did someone else punch him? Did he simply trip? I actually can't even remember, and I'm genuinely telling the truth. The red haze had come down and I went from trying to push him to the door, to throwing him round the kitchen trying to knock him out, just anything to make him stop. My fear was that he would reach out and grab another knife and I'd become a statistic.

All I remember was how it ended.

He was lying on the floor, wide eyed, staring up at the TV which was wobbling precariously above him. We all stopped, thinking it was about to land right on his head. It didn't, it wobbled then stayed in place.

He started crying, and begging Emma – who had now finally given the knife to Niall – to kill him.

If everything could now not get any more surreal, she went over to try and hug him.

He was still sobbing. He jumped up, pushed her away, told us all to leave him alone, and stormed out of the flat.

An eery silence followed for a while. It was broken by someone saying "Has he got his keys?"

His keys? Right enough, that's what we should be concerned about. Him kicking the door in for a second time.

Emma sat down, lit herself a cigarette, apologised and said "I don't even know why I did that" while Niall and I stared at each other trying to comprehend what had just happened.

Of course, Rob had to come back at some point, which he did; storming in and proceeding to trash his bedroom in a drug and drink fueled frenzy, before presumably finally falling asleep, which was probably about the first wink of sleep he'd got in three days.

I lay in bed that night, trying to stay awake. I was convinced I'd be woken up by someone sticking a knife in my chest.

I stayed awake until 8am, when to make the whole thing even more bizarre Rob then had to leave for work.

I got a phone call later that morning from Sarah. She wanted to know why she had a large bump on her eye, while laughing about the wild night SHE'D had.

I still had to live there for another couple of weeks before I moved out. It never got that crazy again, in fact none of us ever spoke about it again.

My friends showed about the smallest amount of sympathy they could. "If you're worried you can stay here for a while........well actually, it'd be a bit crowded."

Moral of the story. If your landlord moves a flatmate into your flat, and you're frightened of the nutter, then tell your landlord immediately. And sleep with a baseball bat under your pillow.

I had many flat mates during my time at and after uni. Everyone had their own wee things which irritate you, its natural, however you always manage to see past it and make the most of it. There was one however which was an 'experience'.

The man in question had the unfortunate attributes of being socially awkward, covered by a freakish amount of body hair and not being the tidiest or cleanest of flatmates. He always kept his room immaculate despite his personal hygiene lacking somewhat, however he never once lifted a finger to help clean the rest of the flat despite leaving everything at his rear end.

An example of this was me returning after spending a week or so staying at my girlfriend at the time (to escape) to find a plate under the couch with was a large blue, black and otherwise indescribable object which had an indescribable stench. It was a Chicken Kiev which he moved under the couch FIVE nights previous, then he hadn't left his room since as he was embarking on a mammoth football manager session on his laptop!

That was, however, surpassed by toilet-gate. A week or so prior to me moving permanently to London he came into my room to confess he had blocked the toilet. Everyone is human, and as a Crohns disease sufferer, I didn't hold it against him. He said he had tried to sort it but couldn't but his dad (supposedly a plumber) was visiting tomorrow and he would do it.

There was a two month period when I had moved to London, but had to pay the Glasgow flat due to the lease. This suited me in a way as my girlfriend (now wife) still lived in Glasgow. I came up to visit about a month and half after I moved and arranged for my girlfriend to meet me at the station, and we would stay at my Glasgow flat that weekend. We arrived back at the flat and the smell at the door was unbelievable. I worked for a waste company and visited every imaginable way of storing waste including land fill, sewage etc and can hand on heart say that it is the most horrible think that my nose has had to encounter.

It turns out the toilet was still blocked, and had been for the entire time I had been away. Worse still, he had continued to live there and kept doing his business in the blocked toilet!!! Honestly was unbelievable!

Craig Forson

8
Passing your course

You mean, you've come here to get a degree?

You're at university. Whether it was your first or last choice, you're there. You've made some friends, settled into your halls, your flatmates are terrific and life is just grand.

If you can find time in the social calender, you may as well spend a wee bit of time on the degree too.

The term "every degree is different" is actually only true to a certain extent. I remember one module, "Management and Organisations". There were three of us one night studying away for it. There was me, a journalism student. Martin, who was on the business studies course. And Craig, doing marketing. Three different courses yet we were all doing the same exam.

Universities work differently. Essentially they are broken into two semesters. Each semester lasts 12 weeks working on three, four or five different modules (depending on your university), followed by an exam period. You might not actually have an exam for that module, it might be marked by in-class assessments, by essays, by presentations, or usually by a mixture (ie one exam, one essay).

Therefore much of the advice I can give will be related to the two degrees I studied on – journalism and sports journalism – but they will generally be handy for any course and any institution.

> *Here's a tip my history teacher gave me in fourth year of high school – I used it for the next seven years of exams and I never failed a single one.*
>
> *Fold an A4 piece of paper in half, twice, so you have four rectangles. Your notes for a single chapter/module/section of that exam should fit into that one small rectangle.*
>
> *If you can't fit your notes in then you haven't learned them well enough.*
>
> *Laura Brannan*

> *I studied BA Journalism at Glasgow Caledonian from 2005-2007. It was a good course and really gives you a good grounding for becoming a successful journalist. I did find it rather boring however because there were a lot of modules that had nothing to do with journalism; modules involving computer spreadsheets and economics, which to me were just nonsense.*
>
> *Add to that the dreaded Shorthand! The bane of my life. I could never get the hang of it and failed the module in second year for my 80 words per minute exam. Despite passing 11 of the 12 modules in the first two years I wasn't allowed to continue. This actually benefited me as by the time I returned to uni in 2009 at UWS in Hamilton I felt more focus and determination to do well than I did as a daft 18 year old.*
>
> *Failing the course at Caledonian has done me no harm at all because at UWS I had the best lecturer any student could wish for. Someone dedicated to her students and who would run through brick walls to make sure you had all the required skills and knowledge to becoming a journalist.*
>
> *Daniel Hayes*

Master the art of sucking up

At Caledonian, there was a guy in our class who clearly put more work in than the rest of us. Not only was he working harder, he made sure the tutors could see he was working harder.

One or two people would comment he was sucking up, playing the teacher's pet. However, this isn't school, it's not a case of working hard to get a gold star or a pat on the head. He knew having the lecturers rate you was going to pay dividends at the later date, and it came as no surprise he was the first from our class to get a job at a newspaper – actually before the course ended – because he had the results in the bag and glowing references to boot.

It was a funny one, because he was actually younger than me. I was the oldest in the class, yet it was him acting like the mature student while maybe I was a little bit too lazy and keen to enjoy the social side too much.

When I started at UWS, I decided to follow his approach. I got the same comments about me, that I was sucking up to the lecturers, but by then I was putting myself and my career first. I was knocking the lecturers door, discussing my work, and looking for more work experience opportunities.

Also by then I was running my own online magazine which did wonders for my CV as it showed I was a self starter. Outside of classes I was grafting away on that, building up a readership, covering events, doing interviews, and getting other writers involved.

I did it because journalism is a dog eat dog world. You don't graduate to a glut of available jobs and it's very much a case where the cream rises to the top. It takes more than your degree to get you ahead in the media world – work experience and references are huge.

My hard work paid off. Not only did I graduate with my degree, my tutor then became my boss, offering me my first full-time role in journalism. I was paid to work on the course, integrating my magazine into the degree to help expand the work experience opportunities for students.

Most employers look for a 2:1 minimum so that's the standard you should set to achieve. This means that no doors are unnecessarily closed on you once you leave.

But, on the other hand, getting a first does not always guarantee you a job.

I chose business studies as a course as I wasn't sure what I wanted to do. The main reason I choose it though was that it had a mandatory placement as part of the degree, this allowed me to get a years' experience as well as an honours degree. This meant that when I graduated I had a job to go to.

Now not everyone will be that lucky, but one thing you have to try to do whilst at uni is pick up those necessary skills and experiences that will make it easier to get a job out of it at the end.

In the first year, it's essentially about passing and learning your subject. So make the most of it. I had a friend who used to say in first year "Every 1% over 40 is a percentage I didn't need, I could have spent longer in the pub".

After first year though, every mark counts towards the final degree.

Martin Allison

Passing the degree

One thing to remember throughout your time at university. No-one fails because they are not clever enough. I have been to university with some incredibly stupid people but they have breezed through their degree.

People fail their degree because they are lazy.

I don't know who most of you are. However, I know this much – you will leave things to the very last minute at uni.

"No I won't" I hear you think. "I'm organised, I work hard, I have a binder where I can store all my notes in alphabetical order. I also have sticky notes - no-one fails at anything when they have sticky notes."

Yes, well done and all that, but listen. You **will** leave things to the last minute. You will be in the library the night before an essay is due panicking that it won't be finished on time. That's just life.

It doesn't matter how many times it is repeated in this book, it won't get through to you, you stubborn so and so.

Don't feel bad though. We all do it, despite vowing that won't happen to us. You will not get through university without at least once sitting up the night before typing away furiously. You won't even be alone, you'll be making 4am phonecalls to your mate to ask how he did his referencing, only to hear he's not done it yet because he's still 2,000 words short.

There will be that point where your essay will be due in at 10am, and at 9.45am you will be in the library printing it off, noticing a mistake, quickly changing it, and printing again, all in a frantic race against the clock.

I've twice handed in essays late and had to sweet-talk the girl at the desk into forgetting the rules and letting me sign it in past the deadline.

You'll do all this at least once because sometimes it's unavoidable. You have weeks where three essays are due and you simply fall behind. It should be avoidable though. You do tend to get at least six weeks notice before your essay is due, and if you start it straight away you'll be fine.

Always try to give yourself a week to write it. Not only because books will be hard to track down, but that way you can write for 2-3 hours in the afternoon, then come back to the library at night and write for another 2-3 hours. You do that for five days, and spend the next two just tidying it up and sorting our your referencing, you'll be fine. Giving yourself 48 hours is not fun. Especially when as soon as it's handed in you've got to then start a second essay that's due in three days later.

You will usually be given some sort of essay guide. You might get a paper copy, you might get it in your lecture notes, or sometimes it'll be available online (universities are starting to use something called "Moodle" now. Some are still using "Blackboard". They don't need an explanation from me because in induction week you'll get that at uni, but essentially they're a way for your lecturer to keep in touch with their students).

The essay guide will always have a structure of how your essay is marked, telling you what areas need to be covered, and what essentially is the difference between a good mark and a bad one.

I used to ignore it at first, but when I actually sat it beside me one day and used it to structure my essay, everything became so much easier. You'll be confident that you've covered every area that needs to be covered, rather than rambling for 2,000 words, none of which are actually getting you any marks.

> *Get someone to proof-read your work, even if you're 100% confident. You will have made a daft mistake that will cost you 5%.*
>
> *They have 100s of exams to mark and they're all written frantically and barely legibly. Give them something different to read for exams and essays - they might reward you for waking them up, because marking is horrible.*
>
> *Always reference an exam, even if you're not sure you got the right study - chances are they won't check, and even if they do you can't lose marks, you just won't gain them.*
>
> *NEVER EVER EVER PLAGIARISE. They know. If you don't have something of your own to say, you shouldn't be at uni.*
>
> Steve Kerr

Referencing is something you will pick up over time at uni. You will get lectures specifically pointing out how to do this so no need for me to explain it in great detail, but I'll give you my simple way of understanding. It's not 100% accurate, but at least ensured I didn't lose too many marks.

Every paragraph you write, you have to prove what you've said is correct. For example, if I wanted to prove this paragraph was correct, I would perhaps point out A.Sully (2013, page 20) proved it was correct when he said that "everything Panda says is generally correct".

The marker will check your list of books and references you will have at the end of the essay, which will have a book titled "Proving Panda right", A.Sully, 2013. Page 20, paragraph three. And now the marker knows where to go to check your reference.

If you do that for every bit you're trying to prove or where you're quoting someone - save for your own opinion - then you'll be okay. Obviously, there are books on referencing, and there are different ways of referencing books, essays, websites, images, etc. Don't reference properly and you'll lose a hell of a lot of marks for it. You can write a good essay but fail because you never proved what you wrote was right, so never dismiss that part of your essay.

Lectures

You'll often be told you don't need to go to lectures. It's generally true. For classes – and these are known as tutorials usually – a register is taken and if you're not at 80% of them you can fail that module just through lack of attendance.

Lectures can sometimes have up to 500 people in the same room, no-one is going to check you're there, and many people take the opportunity to stay in bed during these.

It's obviously beneficial to go, especially the first one, which introduces the module and explains the exams or essays to come. You'll also probably get any booklets handed out in that lecture.

Also, the last lecture will be a round up of everything and gives the biggest hint of what will be in the exam.

Other than that, it's up to you. Really, it depends on how good the lecturer is. Some merely read their notes – notes which you can generally get online. Others will actually go to lengths to explain what is in the notes, and they may put it across in an easy to understand manner.

One lecturer was notorious for having a monotone voice, and his subject wasn't the most exciting either. However, perhaps knowing this, and wishing to keep folk coming to the lectures, he had a wee gimmick that he did every week.

Every lecture, he would spend thirty minutes going through slide after slide, explaining things in a low drawl. Then halfway through the class he would stop, stride forward, and tell everyone a joke! I think people turned up just to hear the joke.

If you go to see a lecturer because you don't understand the coursework, they will usually ask if you were at the lecture, and will be able to work out quickly if you're lying, so try not to miss too many.

> *I did optometry. It was a vocational course, and I was close with everyone in it as there are a lot of hours needed at uni. The course also has a good social side - with football tournaments, pub quizzes, and plenty of nights out.*
>
> *There are very good job opportunities with this course in comparison to teachers, lawyers, journalists - so I am very lucky.*
>
> *Dave McIntosh*

Presentations

You'll generally be put into groups for certain modules, 90% of the time in order to do a class presentation.

The thought of doing these are terrifying to some students, and I wasn't a massive fan of them either if truth be told. However, the key is making sure you're well prepared, that your part of the presentation is well researched and easy to understand, and there's little chance of your tutor interrupting you mid-flow to quiz you in front of the class on your questionable facts.

Therefore, meeting with your group regularly is very important. Make sure you all know what you're doing, and have shared out the work load equally. You'll be a lot less nervous if you know you've got a good presentation, can stand up and read off well prepared notes, and no-one can laugh at your mistakes if you're not making any.

You actually find the whole thing quite rewarding. I remember the nights before I had a class presentation I would be a bit nervous, which is only natural.

Then it would get closer and closer to the point where it'd be ten minutes before class and I was in the toilet, my stomach doing knots, and I'd be staring at the mirror where a pale scared face was screaming back at me.

I'd get to class, hoping that the bad weather had put everyone off and I only had to make the presentation to a mere handful of people. Or even better, the tutor was ill and class was cancelled.

That actually happened once but unfortunately the class got rescheduled for later in the week so our group still had to do the presentation.

Of course, you watch the room fill up, and because some modules are mixed with other courses you don't necessarily know everyone in the room.

You feel sick, like this is going to be the worst day of your life.

When you're up there though it's really not that bad. It's the waiting that's the worst thing. Then that moment when you first stand up and see a room full of people staring back at you, and you want to be anywhere else but there.

Once you're underway, you're going through your power-point, you're reading off your notes, you're making your points clearly, and you maybe look at the lecturer and get a nod of approval - your confidence grows and you finish it feeling quite proud of yourself.

Tell you what, the rest of your day feels great when you've nailed a presentation. There are few better feelings at university (the in-class side of it at least).

That's why you have to do presentations, so you can get better at these things and get more confident.

It's also a way of making you attend more lectures. The idea is the lecture introduces you to a topic, and in your next tutorial you learn it in more depth.

Always make sure you attend the lecture regarding your presentation topic, that's not one to miss. It essentially does half your work for you, as the lecture will usually be one hour, but your presentation generally is a condensed 20 minute version.

Essentially, you're picking out the more important points from the lecture, aided with some of your own research, and presenting that to the class.

> *I studied Social Anthropology with Minor in Modern History. I'm not sure if it was worth it or not yet, but I enjoyed it anyway.*
>
> *I will say that not all classes were necessarily useful, but there's unfortunately no way of telling if it will be or not before you go. So I'd advise to look out for an interval, and escape then.*
>
> *My Master's was better because of the people I was with; it was a smaller group and there was time to bond on a field trip we had to Cumbria. Big regret there actually, don't get so drunk your friends have to consider hospitalising you and your lecturer has to take you to get a hangover breakfast next morning. Low point. Do take advantage of field trip opportunities though, definitely a good idea for getting to know people on your course better.*
>
> *Ruth Cowden*

Now there is more detailed reading out there on how to make a good presentation, but I'll give you a quick hint for what I generally did.

Put bullet points on the screen, and read your notes to explain them in more detail. When I say notes, I don't mean stand with your head down reading out a long essay. Have notes in front of you to remind you what to say if you forget your train of thought, but you should know the information you're telling anyway, so you should be able to confidently explain what it is.

A good idea if you have time and are particularly organised is for your group to meet up an hour before class and have everyone stand up and do their part of the presentation to each other. It will help you memorise what you want to say, and also give your group members a chance to point out any mistakes.

Don't just pick random statistics to read out without knowing what relevance they actually make to the point you're putting across, because your lecturer will simply interrupt you, question you on it, and you'll turn bright red as the class giggles.

Don't do the opposite, which many do, where they put paragraphs (or even worse, a mass jumble of words) on the screen, and expect the class to read it. While they're reading it, you essentially read bullet points and say things like "here's an explanation of the change in market trends" and then awkwardly point to the screen, expecting them to read something you clearly copy and pasted from somewhere and haven't even learned yourself.

It's the cowards way out and also doesn't come across well, especially when there's silence while you wait for people to read the mountain of information you've put up.

Here's the mistake people make. They think that no-one in the class cares, so they're not really paying attention. Three of us did a presentation on the then chancellor Gordon Brown's budget. It wasn't the most riveting of things to study, and as hard as we worked to present it in an easy to understand way I doubt many of the class were on the edge of their seats.

However, even if no-one in our class were really paying attention, the tutor was listening to every word, reading everything on the screen, and comparing all our "facts" with his knowledge of information in his head. You're standing up in front of the class, but you're really presenting to the man or woman who will be marking your efforts.

As I said, preparation is key. If you have to rush off from group meetings, or miss them altogether because you've a shift at work, then you might get an unwanted reputation as someone who can't be relied upon.

You might have a relaxed attitude to attending lectures, but don't let your group mates down – you'll find yourself being avoided when it comes to creating groups later on because you'll be seen as a slacker.

It wasn't uncommon to see people turn up on the day of the presentation and ask their mates what they were meant to be doing. In fact, one unbelievable story happened in our class.

One module we had in third year, we were split into five groups, and each week all five had to make a weekly twenty minute presentation.

One guy (not in my group thankfully) was so scared of standing up in front of everyone he thought he would get out of it by avoiding his group members until the day of the class.

His thinking behind it was that if he turned up with nothing prepared, then he didn't have anything to actually read out, so could stand at the back and let everyone else do the work.

He actually got away with it for a few weeks before his group got fed up of his antics. So, they split the presentation into four parts, with three of them having a quarter each, and set aside a part for him; which you can imagine was the most difficult part.

He turned up minutes before the tutorial, having made no effort to contact anyone in the seven days previous, and was shocked to be told he would have to stand up in front of the class, unprepared, and present a part of the presentation.

He had no notes, nothing to put on the power-point presentation, and in truth no idea what he would say.

Unashamedly, he put on his coat and walked out! Imagine having him in your group?

> *I studied fashion marketing. It wasn't worth it in the sense that no one in my class got a decent job from it, but that's not to say I wish I hadn't done it. It led to me doing a masters at Strathclyde University, and then being offered a Phd and as such could have (if I hadn't got knocked up!) led to a lecturing job at Strathclyde.*
>
> *Saying that my masters was in Supply Chain Management as I quickly realised that nothing comes from studying fashion. My advice for passing it is to get all the nights out and fun out the way in the first two years as you certainly can't be doing it in third and fourth year. Also, focus on learning to write well; anyone can learn a subject, but the key for good marks is always in a well written report. Of course the dissertation is the biggest report you'll ever write, and if you can't write no matter whats in it, it won't score well.*
>
> *I also was quite OCD about my notes from uni and kept them all in pukka pads, colour coordinated, which took forever but really paid off for exams as my revision was all ready for me. I used notes from first year in fourth year exams and it saved on reading.*
>
> *And avoid group work at all times, its a pain in the arse and never ever works well.*
>
> *Natalie McDougall*

Never listen to a lecturer who tells you "not to worry"

So, here's me with all my advice, and yet the sharp ones amongst you will have noticed I started my degree at Glasgow Caledonian University, and finished it at the University of the West of Scotland.

I happily went through two years of journalism, passing all the modules. However, four of us became unstuck with a subject known as "shorthand".

Shorthand is like learning a new language. It's essential for journalists because it teaches you to write words in what are basically small symbols. It's useful for doing phone interviews or covering a court case where you can't record anything.

All the essay advice above was useless because the shorthand exam is about speed. My problem was I couldn't do it fast enough.

Now, in fairness, I practiced and failed. If I'd practiced more, I would have passed the exam because I was never far away from doing it (and eventually did pass the exam at UWS when I finally knuckled down).

However, myself and three others who had yet to pass it were told throughout the summer holidays to not worry about it. No-one had ever failed the degree having failed shorthand before, and it was seen as an extra module, a bonus added on to the degree.

As long as we passed everything else, we were assured we would be heading into third year.

Problem is though, every other student in the years before us had sat shorthand in third and fourth year. With it being considered an extra module, not even part of the course, if you failed, you just failed shorthand. However, they still gave you your degree. Some journalism courses don't even have shorthand on the curriculum.

Our year was the first where they had taught you shorthand at the start of the course. So, we had started it in first year, with the resits running into second year.

Now, they had four students who'd only passed two years and would be going through the rest of the course having never passed the module. They were not entirely sure what to do with that.

We would have made their lives a lot easier had we all just passed. We didn't, despite four lazy attempts. So, after a summer of telling us we would be fine, we got a letter one day written in small print at the bottom telling us we'd failed the course.

Two of the four couldn't complain, they'd barely turned up for class and had failed plenty more modules.

Myself and one other though, Danny, only had shorthand to pass, we couldn't help but feel a little hard done by. Apart from the shorthand we were actually good students. We turned up more often than many others on the course, put more effort into the exams and essays, and had good marks to show for it.

If a tutor had just taken us aside and said "look, you fail this and you're off the course" we would have treated the situation as serious as we should have, got to work, and I've little doubt we both would have nailed the resit.

If you find yourself like us though, well, then you still can't complain really. It was still our fault for not taking the exam seriously. If we'd put the effort in, we'd have passed.

You could suggest the course leader was still in the wrong because he had suggested it didn't really matter when, in the end, it clearly did.

Really though, it wasn't up to him to give us a kick up the arse. By the end of second year it's up to you to take responsibility. It was our fault, a bit of laziness over one module and we were off a degree we were both flying in.

However, once we'd got over feeling sorry for ourselves, we went and spoke to the careers teacher. She informed us we just had to complete a replacement module, and we could leave with a Diploma, or "Diploma of Higher Business (DipHE)", which is considered just an inch better than a HND on account the award comes on a university course as opposed to college.

So, we stayed on for another few months, got the diploma, didn't graduate with the degree we'd came for but had something to show for the two years we had done.

Now me, I was happy enough, went to Ayia Napa and when I came back I moved home to Aberdeen.

If I was being honest, perhaps because of my age, I was starting to think more about work and getting a job than another two years studying, and I was becoming more interested in making my magazine and website work than I was in having a degree.

By 2008 I would have been going into fourth year at that point anyway which I wasn't even sure if I wanted to do, and by then the student life calms down as people worry about dissertations.

So I was pretty okay with it. It was a year later though when it hit me.

There were a lot of good people in our class, people I knew would go on to have long successful careers in journalism. There were also a lot who I knew I was far better than, and there I was looking at everyone's graduation photos, seeing them all standing in their gowns grinning like Cheshire cats, and I felt like I'd missed out on something.

Other people I'd met in halls were all posting their graduation photos, and I felt a bit left out.

I also remember a comment my dad said to me just after I got my Higher results. He said I'd be the first person in our family to go to university. I thought it'd be a shame if I was the first to go, but not the first to get a degree.

I knew then it would eat away at me for the rest of my days if I didn't go back, do one more year, and get my degree. It was personal pride more than anything.

As luck had it, UWS were starting a sports journalism course in 2009, offering first and third year entry. The course was started by one of my old lecturers from Caley who remembered both Danny and I and knew we were capable of more. She gave us direct entry to third year, a second chance, and it was one we didn't throw away.

I actually enjoyed going back. Being a new course there were only six of us in the class and we all socialised together. We also had a rivalry going with the journalism course who we shared a lot of classes with, and took great pride in getting higher marks than them.

Our course leader was proud too because we were showing the university was right to have a sports journalism course, and that rather than be behind the general journalism students we were ahead of them.

A year later I had a degree in BA Sports Journalism. I could have stayed on and did honours too but I felt I had done what I had to do; gone back and proved I could get the degree, got my graduation photo in the gown, and could now go back drinking with all my old pals from uni without being embarrassed that they had got degrees and I'd failed.

The whole episode taught me a few life lessons.

First, if you fail an exam then work twice as hard to pass it the next time. Don't keep making the same mistakes I did by not upping the work rate.

I also never asked for help from anyone, be it tutors or friends. That was another mistake. I should have roped in friends and got them to help me practice. I was sitting the exam after months of not even bothering to practice – looking back I deserved to fail the course.

Secondly, if you've failed, and someone else has too, and they have a pretty relaxed attitude to it, that doesn't mean you should follow them. The four of us in our class who failed, none of us were bothered so none of us "rallied the troops" as it were.

If other people are in the same boat then you worry about it less than you should, a "we're all in this together" mentality. That's not much use when you're no longer on the course.

Thirdy, never leave your career in the hands of a tutor who perhaps has hundreds of students to think about. A lot of the time you're just a name on a sheet of paper. You will find some who will go that extra mile for you and give you that extra encouragement. Others you feel would rather be somewhere else than listening to your problems.

What you should be trying to do is get to know them. If you've not had a conversation with your lecturer at least once a month, then you're not talking to them enough.

Failure isn't the end of the world. It is preferable to pass of course, but there's always a plan B out there. Always.

My plan B actually worked out well because I graduated into a job at the university that I would never have got without studying at UWS. It's easy for me to say now, but they say everything happens for a reason – maybe me not passing shorthand was for the best.

And at UWS I did eventually pass shorthand. I don't think I've ever used it since.

My degree was Environmental Management and Planning – I would not recommend it in the slightest.

Best tip would be after a year or so of doing it, if your not enjoying it get out and change degrees. Don't get caught up on having the craic, you can have that anywhere.

Don't get me wrong my degree has got me a job doing something that I like, but there would have been a much easier route if I decided to change universities.

Andy Laverty

I did a marketing degree. It's worth it because I couldn't have got a job in my chosen career, though in general any business degree would do the same if not better.

I wish I had done more practical work like photoshop, indesign, dreamweaver, SEO etc... all of which would of been much more applicable to my career development.

Get as much experience in work as possible (from second year on, first years is party time, if you're getting A's you're not partying enough). Maybe learn another language if you can too.

Craig Dunlop

9
Relationships

The University of Life. This will be a short chapter, or at least it should be. The longer it is the more depressing it'll be for those of you coming to university who are already in a couple.

Long distance relationships are tough. Relationships through a phone or laptop aren't a lot of fun. It will also increase your homesickness a lot.

It also works the other way. You can meet someone at university, but then when you both graduate you might be going your separate ways.

You'll probably give yourself a much easier time by staying single. However, I'm not here to have an argument with cupid (though the little rascal owes me). If you love your girlfriend or boyfriend, then you know what, stick together. At least give it a go. Who am I to tell you it won't last?

Give it a chance – but do expect it to be hard. Don't start university then moan that you didn't realise how hard it was going to be.

I have to be honest though. I knew of ten people in halls who came to university in a couple. Not one of them lasted until the end of the degree.

Most of them cheated within the first few months. I think it's the feeling that you're missing out if you're in a couple, that you need to devote a lot of time to that person when all the single people are out embracing their new life.

I was seeing one girl, who had decided to break up with her boyfriend of three years. Her move to university had convinced her she wasn't missing him that much and the relationship was never going to last the four years she was away.

The girl, to her credit, didn't want to break up with him over the phone. I felt bad about it, and I felt even worse when I slipped round to her flat to say hello and the poor guy was sat in the kitchen because he was visiting for the weekend, and he hadn't yet been given the bad news.

Even worse, her flatmates introduced me to him – he was a fellow Aberdeen fan, so there was us shaking hands and chatting about the Dons. I had to be rude and leave, I couldn't sit and chat with a guy who was getting dumped partly because of me.

It wasn't uncommon though. You would pull girls and then a week later see them with their boyfriends from back home, and you'd give each other a sheepish grin.

> *Don't ever get a girlfriend or boyfriend at uni. That's just stupid.*
>
> *The only thing worse would be keeping your own high school boy/girlfriend. They will get horribly jealous, you will never see them, you'll feel guilty for enjoying yourself, you'll drift apart and they will violently hate every single one of your friends.*
>
> *I only know one couple who stayed together from high school and they were possibly the most boring people I've ever met in my life.*
>
> *You will never be this good looking, you will never know so many people, you will never drink so cheaply, you will never have more of an opportunity to know what you like.*
>
> *Relationships come later. Unfortunately so does the confidence to recognise all of that.*
>
> *Steve Kerr*

I think in all honesty the long distance relationship thing is worse for the person who is left back home. The year before I left for Glasgow, I had a girlfriend studying at Edinburgh uni and I missed her because I was at home, living in a small town and working a boring job.

When I would go down to visit her, there she was sharing a flat with five friends living the student lifestyle.

The worst part was always driving home and going back to the place where I was stuck living with the parents, most of my friends all had jobs so weren't available to go out drinking the same way you can as students, and everything just feels a little less exciting in comparison.

If I had been at university myself at the time, I don't think it'd have been as bad, as I'd have had something else to distract me.

We broke up eventually, not because of the long distance thing. It was more to do with how the planets are aligned I suppose, we were up against it from the very start. You see, I was a Sagittarius, and she was a miserable wee cow.

I'm sure your relationship will survive if it's really meant to be.

> *When I started at Lincoln (I went to uni there for a year straight out of school and dropped out) I accidentally peed in a girls mouth at freshers week.*
>
> *She was giving me a blow-job, but kept going after I'd finished. I tried to get her off me but she was adamant she was still going.*
>
> *I felt something like another shot, but actually it was about three litres of VK orange coming out in spurts. She swallowed the lot.*
>
> *Next time I visited her she started to nosh me off and then said "I'm not swallowing this time". I kept that to myself to save her embarrassment, but then she turned out to be an arsehole so I took great pleasure in telling people about it.*
>
> *Anonymous!*

Don't let a relationship get in the way of making friends. There were people who went home every weekend to see their partner. There were those who hid in their room for days with a visiting boyfriend or girlfriend and therefore didn't socialise with anyone.

When these people inevitably break-up, they've got no mates, because they didn't make any.

They also have so many regrets because they never went out and enjoyed themselves as often as they could. This is your opportunity to go on so many cheap nights out, with so many single friends, be able to shake off a hangover so easily and have so much free time to just do whatever you want.

When you graduate, many of your uni friends will leave to go back home. Those that stay can only do so if they've got a job, so you see them at the weekends.

Then they get themselves into a couple, they have kids, and presumably you start doing the same, and eventually you can actually count the amount of nights out clubbing you've had in a year. A mad night is staying out past 1am.

Don't waste it at university. You don't have to go and sleep with everyone you see to have a good time, but throw yourself into uni life.

Socialise, join clubs, and hey if you pull, you pull. As long as he or she back home doesn't know about it then no-body gets hurt. If you do start sleeping with someone then maybe your relationship isn't that strong anyway.

> *One embarrassing story I remember is that I pulled this really hot girl in a club when I was like 18, and she asked if I wanted to go back to hers. For some reason instead of saying "Yes that would be great", I replied "Na sorry I'm staying over my mates house". Still don't know why.*
>
> Ben Archibald

If you are looking for actual advice on how to pull, well there's books for that sort of thing. However, here's some things from my locker. I'm no pick-up artist, being truthful most of these are generally things I've learned from the many mistakes I did make.

Freshers week is the easiest time to pull. Everyone is out to make friends so everyone chats away willingly, and you're not going to get rejected very much.

Take advantage of that, you will never in your life have as much confidence and such a success rate with striking up conversations with hot 18 year olds. It gets much harder after this, trust me. That girl who is chatting away to you now might ignore you in six months when she has an army of mates, so make your move while she's wendy no pals.

Get your dancing shoes on. People go on the dance floor for two reasons, to dance and to pull. Don't walk around trying to grind someone from behind (and I'm not just talking to the lads here). Just dance with your mates, make eye contact with someone you like, and smile. If they smile back, go dance with them, and make your move.

Don't spend ages dancing with someone who hasn't kissed you. If it's been ten minutes, then they're just dancing with you to be polite. You might think you're laying the groundwork but you're probably not. If you think they're just shy then you're going to have to make the first move. You need to learn the difference between someone who's shy and someone who's not interested quickly, otherwise you'll be buying them drinks all night for no reason.

That's another rule, don't buy anyone drinks all night. I get girls coming up to me in a club and asking me to buy them a drink, and it doesn't matter who they are or how hot they are I always say no. Pop their ego a little otherwise they'll walk all over you.

Besides, I wouldn't walk up to a bloke I don't know and say "Alright mate, you gonna buy me a drink". If I did and it worked I wouldn't think very highly of him, I'd be going back to my mates and laughing about it, and that's what a girl will think of you if you're queuing up to shower her with gifts all the time.

Also, clearly, don't get too drunk, and don't go out in a grey or brown t-shirt that's likely to be different shades of sweat. Doesn't matter if you're good looking or ugly, make an effort and the opposite sex will notice.

Don't expect people to be desperate to hop into bed with you just because you're both students. Likewise, don't feel pressured into sleeping with someone either, especially if you're a girl and it's freshers week.

Being honest, and I'm sorry lads I'm letting our side down here, but my advice to any girl would be to not sleep with anyone in freshers week. Remember my flatmate? Don't let that be one of the first memories people have of you.

If you are going to sleep around, don't let everyone know about it. Tell your close mates, but you don't want everyone knowing, especially the opposite sex. That works for girls and boys. Having a reputation might ruin your chances with someone else.

We all had the pal who was "A nice guy but a bit of a slag." That description hurt him at the time, but I think he secretly likes it now.

Don't let people tell you uni is all about sex – it's about having fun, laughing out loud, telling stories, making memories…and you do that with friends, not one night stands.

Laura Brannan

When you meet someone you really like, don't delay in asking them out.

Students at university tend to have a lot of friends, and they're also going out a lot.

They are meeting new people every day, so thinking you can put a few months in making friends and doing some ground work isn't actually a good idea.

If you like them, ask to do something, just the two of you. Usually, the penny drops pretty quickly - if not with them then their friends - and they'll realise it's an unofficial date at least, so walking them home you can actually just tell them you like them and it won't come as a huge shock.

If they make an excuse not to go with you, don't take it as rejection just yet.

A mistake I made was that I confused a girl being shy with rejection. That wasn't the case.

I later heard she had never been on a date before because she'd been dating her boyfriend since school, and just didn't feel comfortable and would rather we had went out in a group.

So if they say no, then arrange something as a group or with another couple and see if you have any better luck.

If they say no again, then that's when you take your hint and move on.

Apart from freshers week, the best place to meet people is in halls and at work.

I worked in a nightclub, and the staff generally got together with other staff members. Is it awkward if something happens? Not when you work in a nightclub, and not when everyone is at it anyway.

The awkward ones were the people who weren't at it!

That's my advice on getting started. The actual art of keeping a girl and getting a ring on their finger is something I'm still learning with you my friend.

One particular story which I've been sworn not to tell any names...

Basically, a few of us were out in Edinburgh and we met up with this group of girls who also had a booth in the same club as us. After a few drinks we got talking to them and my friend took a fancy with this one particular girl. She told him she runs for Great Britain, none of us recognised her so we assumed she was an up and coming athlete, but were all impressed.

Anyway, as things happened we all ended up back at one of my friends' flats. The particular friend who was interested in this athlete took a bottle of wine and the girl to his room while we stayed in the lounge playing drinking games.

In the morning, I was up early sitting at the table as I heard my friend show the lady out the door. He entered the room and told me the nights events...

The two had gone into his room, finished the bottle of wine, took it to the next level and he then took his clothes off and got into bed.

She followed, took her clothes off and then sat on the bed as she took one of her legs off. Turns out that this woman was a Paralympic sprinter, with only one leg.

Anonymous

10
Mature students

Dealing with an age old problem.

Since starting university, and being "grandad" to everyone, I've had to go through every birthday with cards wishing me "Happy 30th." They became such a regular occurrence that the dread of actually reaching my 30's left me long before I eventually reached the big three zero. I'd already turned 30 six times previous!

Being the mature student amongst teenagers at university is something I was a bit concerned about before I started.

I wondered how long I would get away with hiding my age before eventually having to admit it. It lasted hardly any time at all, it was one of those questions you find people ask you on your first day at university as an ice breaker.

I didn't want to lie and pretend I was 18 and the same age as everyone else, but I didn't want to say I was 23 and up to six years older than the people I was meeting.

I'm sure many of you who are mature students will be toying with the same dilemma ahead of university.

In the end, it was a piece of cake. At the first party I attended on the first night of halls, the room went quiet while a rather loud girl asked three of us who were leaning against the kitchen worktop how old we all were.

The whole room stayed hushed when I announced I was 23. I hadn't even said I was actually only a few short months from being 24, but the shock value was already there.

The loud girl seemed stunned, before asking bizarrely "Why are you here?"

What can you say to that? What am I supposed to do, put my beer down, apologise for intruding on the young 'uns fun, and slump off home?

I said "Probably the same reason you're here."

A few people laughed, she smiled and said "Fair enough", and that was that.

I expected more, I thought they'd probe further, dismiss me as too old, avoid the creepy older guy, but what I found in them first few weeks was a reaction I didn't expect. They liked having an older person about.

You see, as long as you're not trying to be everyone's dad, everyone quite likes an older friend.

My age was a constant butt of jokes within my eventual group of pals. Any time we were at a party, or got talking to people in a nightclub, you could count the seconds before they announced "Try and guess how old he is."

To be fair though, I never looked 23, I looked 17, and that was what the gimmick was. The fact I was older than everyone else never bothered anyone, at least not that I know of. Even when I was 28 and in my final year at the University of West of Scotland, it was never an issue.

People, girls it seemed, quite liked having a more mature person about. Unfortunately that didn't describe me at all but it took them a few weeks to work that out.

> *I found it surprisingly difficult to speak to people or make friends in my actual classes as nobody really talked before or after lectures that much. I never made any decent friends in my uni classes – my best friends were all from my accommodation and jobs.*
>
> *Ruth Cowden*

And so my friends, if you're an older gent or woman, my tip to you is to embrace being the mature student, rather than trying to hide it.

At the end of the day, you're a student just like everyone else. You've perhaps moved to a new city, and you're experiencing everything for the first time like they are – except maybe losing your virginity, or getting drunk for the first time.

Essentially though you're all going through the same experiences together, and I never really felt older than anyone else, I always felt like I was the same age.

Even now I feel the same age as the people I went to university with. I went on a stag weekend with friends I'd went to school with, and I just wasn't on the same wavelength at all. University to them was something that happened so long ago they could barely remember it, they were in highly paid jobs, married with kids. There I was saying I had just graduated and was in my first proper job.

You're only as old as you feel, so I plead with you, don't avoid halls because you think you're too old for it.

Now, I suppose there's a difference between being 23 and having your mates 5/6 years younger than you, and being 40 and having everyone not even half you age.

However, even if you're in your 40's, unless you're already happily married, I'd still recommend halls. Obviously in a different capacity, perhaps fresher parties won't be your thing by that age, and chances are you won't have the patience for living with flatmates who have no idea how to keep a place tidy.

There is still the experience of living with foreign students, most of which will be well into their 20's anyway so a little older.

> *Befriend at least one tutor. Amongst a load of cretin there is usually one nice teacher who will actually be genuinely helpful and friendly to you. Make the most of that relationship, it will come in handy.*
>
> *Laura Brannan*

Most older students probably will prefer to get a flat, and that's absolutely fine, but don't forget the whole idea of socialising. Make sure you still join clubs, go for a few drinks with course mates, and accept invites now and then to nights out and parties.

It's university, it's unique, and you will generally only be a fresher once.

If anyone does have a problem with you being older than them, ask them to do something. Ask them to remember your conversation when they do eventually get to your age, and ask them to evaluate their life.

They could be working a boring 9-5 job because the degree they studied didn't lead to the job of their dreams. They could be stuck with kids, a horrible wife/husband, perhaps a mountain of debt from the student loan and the mortgage they're now paying.

Ask them to remember that at your age, you were at university, without a care in the world. Which one of you spent them years having the most fun?

> *One party I'll always remember for being just weird. A group of Fine Art students transformed their rented flat into a exhibition space, knocked through walls, all sorts, without telling their landlord. They had a party one night and, obviously, word spread, eventually leading to their flat being packed full with people filling the close as well trying to get in. The sweat from the sheer amount of people in the flat caused the wallpaper to start peeling off, someone jumped on the fireplace and ripped it off the wall. Then the police appeared and everyone ran out and across the road into another flat. Needless to say the Fine Art folk found themselves evicted soon after.*
>
> *Ashley Johnston*

11
Through the good times and the bad

Sometimes, it can all get a bit too much. We're not infallible. University, and life itself, can be tough. There are plenty things that will stress you out and we all deal with these situations differently.

You might be young, living away from home for the first time, and simply homesick.

You might be mature student and not adjusting to the change in lifestyle.

Perhaps, you'll be lonely. Or maybe you're not getting enough time to yourself - irked by your noisy flatmates.

You could be overworked. Struggling with the course. Worrying about money.

University will throw plenty of challenges your way and inevitably something will get to you eventually.

Don't ever try and deal with things on your own, there is always, ALWAYS, someone who can help you with whatever problem you have.

I'm no expert on every problem, but I will try and help you through some of them that I know will crop up for many of you, and try and give as much advice as I can.

In an earlier chapter I admitted for, just a day or two at least, I felt a little homesick. It came on twice. Once I was lying in bed, in a room that just didn't feel like mine, and suddenly being away from home comforts started to register. I just missed my own bed to be honest.

Most of us don't appreciate the work our parents do to keep us safe and in as much luxury as they can afford. Stepping out of your comfort zone to fend for yourself can be hard to adjust to.

The second time I was at a party. I actually bonded with that group really well eventually, and some of them are still my best friends today. That night though I just remember sitting there while everyone was laughing and joking, and I was struggling slightly to fit in. I was missing my mates back home where I didn't worry about saying the wrong thing – if I said something stupid to them they'd laugh, if I said it here they'd think I was weird. At least, that was what was going through my head anyway.

To get through it, I just did. I just just got over it. I just got comfortable with my surroundings and my new group of friends, and everything just became easier. I stopped worrying what people thought of me and just got drunk, told rubbish jokes, and it just clicked.

That's not particular good advice really, "I just did it". However, you do. There isn't a magic formula. You just keep hanging around with the same friends, and eventually you feel more comfortable in their company, and you start being you around them.

It's funny, you worry someone will slag you off. However, when someone does, it's actually a relief. It shows you're comfortable enough with each other to laugh at everyone, and you take it in the good spirit it's intended.

So when we stopped trying to be nice to each other, and just started being ourselves....that's when I felt at home. After that, I never got a whiff of homesickness again.

For you though, it might be different. Talk to someone, tell your flatmates or new friends you're feeling homesick if you are. You'll generally find someone who will go out of their way to help you settle in. You'll probably find someone else in the same boat.

TIP: Having a degree is only one thing after you graduate. When you're looking for a job, everyone has a degree.

You need to be able to show that you were involved in other things too.

Work experience is invaluable, as not only does it give you a head start, it also gives you references too.

However, don't fall into the trap of being taken advantage of. Many companies will have you working the same hours as full-time staff with paying you for it.

A year's internship might be worth the same on your CV as one month.

If you are lonely, try and immerse yourself into your new life, and remember there is no better place than university to expand your social circle. Look at the list of clubs available, and try and join one. Don't just join the gym, join a class there where you can meet someone else. If you're getting a part-time job, don't go for one where you'll be working alone or with people not in your age group – get a job in a sociable place where you're working with similar people to you.

Try and go out. Even if you're not a drinker or don't like late nights, it's not healthy to be a social pariah who stays in and shuns everyone. You'll find people will be patient with you to a point, and we all had the "quiet" flatmate, our own one included, who wouldn't come out. We'd put some effort in, knock their doors, invite them out. Eventually, you'll only hear "no" so many times and just stop trying.

Try and accept an invitation, even if you won't stay long. Let them know you appreciate them making the effort. People don't mind if you're a quiet person who doesn't talk much, you don't have to be the life and soul of the party, but you can at least join the party once in a while otherwise everyone will move on and forget about you.

If you're not the one having problems with stress, there's a good chance someone you know is. It is amazing from putting this book together and talking to people how many times people have admitted they were either in tears - or close to tears - in private, but never spoke out. Especially guys who want to give the impression they couldn't care less. Little things, even fancying a girl who lives upstairs from you, can be hard to deal with and people deal with it in different ways.

I'm not going to name them, but we knew of someone in first year halls who was, frighteningly, cutting herself. I never did find the reason they were doing it, but they obviously were in a dark place.

In halls there will usually be a councillor or someone similar who is nearby. We couldn't convince her to go see him, so we went ourselves and explained what was going on, without giving her name. Obviously all he could do was give us a leaflet and ask us to sit down with the person and either get them to talk to us, or at least be convinced to go see the councillor.

If you're in that position, and you think someone you know is struggling, try talking to them, or at least go and speak to someone who can help.

On social media these days, namely Twitter and Facebook, there are so many people who do selfishly (in my opinion) constantly crave attention by posting every single complaint and irritation they have. We all know that person, because we all have them on our time-line. Because of them it's easy to dismiss a genuine concerning comment as just another spoilt brat posting nonsense for attention. But get to know your friends, try and spot what is a post that maybe is a wee bit out of character. It doesn't take much to reply asking how they are.

Most of us will have a bad period, rather than four years of depression, but for the most part university is the best thing you'll ever do.

If you really hate it though. If you really aren't enjoying the course, and aren't enjoying where you're living, then it is never too late to do something about it. Just don't make hasty decisions. It's better to have given something a chance than to not even have bothered.

You will make mistakes, you will have the odd regret, and you will have bad days. That's life though, you've got to take the good times with the bad, and if you do university right then the good times will far outweigh the bad.

I can only help you so much though. From now on, it's up to you.

Making the best of it

It's simple. Be sociable and make as many friends as you can. You don't need to be the most popular person on campus, but having a close wee group of friends is all you need.

You don't have to be out every night, but make sure you are going out. You don't want to do four years of uni, look back, and have no stories to tell.

Strike a balance between work, study and play. Be organised so you can spread your uni work out. Don't let a boss take advantage of you and give you too many shifts – just do what you need.

Likewise, it's good to join up to clubs and societies, but don't let them take over your calender either. Don't join everything. Some days you just need a day where you can stay in bed late, or a free weekend where you can go home and visit the parents.

You will generally work over two semesters. The first semester runs until December, and then you will have exams in January. Then from February onwards you do another set of modules with exams in May or June. Some universities are different but that's the general rule.

Things quieten down around exam time because people have essays due, or are studying for exams.

In first year though a whole group of us got lucky. I don't think I had a single exam, or if I did it was very early on. My mates only had one at most too and they were all early on in the exam timetable, so we found ourselves with three weeks off before the second semester started. Result.

We put the student loan to good use. Four of us booked a week in Manchester. It's always good to get away, and Manchester is a cheap holiday. It was just good to get a change of scenery, try some new clubs. We went to a Man Utd-Blackburn game, and it was a good lads week away.

Likewise, you can't go wrong by booking a cheap lads holiday abroad, and five of us went club 18-30 to Malia one summer. Of course it's not so good when you get so drunk on the first night you can't remember half of it, and spend three days ill not sure if you've simply got the world's worst hangover, picked up a bug, or have had your drink spiked and are paying the price.

Either way that week in Malia probably wasn't my greatest seven days but I managed to more than make up for it at the end of my time at Glasgow Caledonian.

I went to work in Ayia Napa, Cyprus, for four months. I worked as a barman and a PR, soaking up the sun by day, partying for free at night. The money is awful but that's not why you go. You go because it's free drink, free entry to all the clubs, partying all night, and waking up on a beach with the sun on your back (maybe sleep in the shade though because sun burn is horrible).

Now that was just one thing I decided to do, but there are plenty of other things you can do over summer. Another friend went to America and worked in Disneyland. Others worked in skiing camps. Others went and got jobs relevant to their degree.

Some more graduated and went travelling round the world, giving themselves a year before looking for a job. Australia I hear pay great salaries – just a shame it's so expensive to get there and back in the first place.

Use your time wisely, because this is your opportunity to do what you want, when you want.

Now if I mention to my parents I fancy another four month stint in Cyprus I get the death stare and reminded I've a mortgage to pay for (I might secretly go one day and never tell them).

I've friends with kids now who can never just go off on a whim. Others are married.

Sit down and make sure you're doing everything you want to do. Don't regret the degree, or where you're moving to.

Make sure you're going to have enough money to get by, but look for ways to top up the party fund.

This book is a guide, it's not a rulebook though. I'm simply giving you some tips. It's your life and what I find a lot of fun might be incredibly boring to you, and vice versa.

You don't have to plan your life out for the next four years, but have a wee list of things you want to do. Maybe make up a wee bucket list and vow to get them all done before you graduate.

I was going to actually write a bucket list and put it at the end of this book and have you tick it off over the years of your degree. Then I realised that would be wrong because it's not for me to tell you what you should be doing over the next four years. Create your own bucket list.

The only thing in this book I'm asking you to do is try, if you can, to live in university halls in first year because I'm confident 99% of you would regret it if you don't.

Everything else is just some advice and a retelling of my own experiences.

Go off and enjoy university, and be proud of it. Every single graduate is jealous of you, because we'd all love to go back and relive it.

We had so many funny stories. We has a water fight in the flat. Someone ripped my shower off the wall, and the whole flat smelt like cabbage for a month.

Pretending to nightclubs that you're experiencing morning sickness to stop from being chucked out. Being sick all over myself in broad daylight in front of 100 school kids. Inventing drinking games and waking up outside. Being conned by a junkie into paying £20 for a bottle of Smirnoff filled with water. Having a jelly fight and subsequently having to paint the walls to hide it. Doing the uni challenge, thinking its okay to get naked and lick cream off a stranger on a stage. The list goes on and on.

Life without uni is no where near as much fun, or as sociable. Hence why I went to do a masters, and then a phd! Its a once in a lifetime experience that is different for everyone, but you don't know how good it is until it's gone.

Contrary to belief, I don't think I'll ever have as much disposable income as I did as a student, and I'll probably never work as hard again either! People who haven't done it, and I mean fully done it with moving away from home, will never understand what they've missed out on. And although I don't know anyone who got a job from it - besides pharmacists and opticians - I also don't know anyone who regrets it. I don't think I could go back to that way of life now, I'm too domesticated now, but it was AMAZING while it lasted.

Natalie McDougall

Good luck

This is it. I'm done with you now, off you go.

Thanks for taking the time to read this book. I hope it's been useful and at least once during your time at university you remember something you read here and make the right decision.

By all means, contact me if you have any other questions and I'll try my best to help, and I'd appreciate comments on the book to see how helpful it actually was.

E-mail a.southwick@ymail.com, or follow me on twitter @a_southwick.

God bless.

Printed in Great Britain
by Amazon